Contents

Chapter Four

Ethnicity   51

Chapter Five

Structure and Conflict   68

Bibliography   85

Index   87

Preface

Perhaps it is reasonable to assume that most readers of this book share our view that racism is vicious and unacceptable, but sadly it is far from extinguished in our society. Race problems take many forms (racially-motivated assaults, harsh treatment by public authorities, the dogged persistence of racial disadvantage) but in each case they demand our attention as caring citizens. In addition to our concern for the human casualties of racism, we believe that the discipline of sociology can make an important contribution to the far-ranging debates about race issues. This might seem a surprising claim, since critics frequently lament the relatively undeveloped state of this branch of sociology. Nevertheless, an increasing number of sociologists are adopting professional interests in this field, and inevitably this has enriched the available literature. Clearly it is not possible to cover the entire range of relevant findings, ideas, theories and controversies, but we hope that the selection offered in this book will at least make the larger body of work more accessible.

The material is arranged according to the following plan: In chapter one we describe some preliminary models before investigating the scientific and popular meanings of race. Then, in chapter two, we chart the migration processes and patterns which have shaped Britain's present status as a truly multi-racial, multi-cultural society. Also, we outline the assumptions of the 'immigrant-host model' as a means of understanding the social reception of the successive waves of migrants. Contrary to the rather optimistic expectations of this model, racial prejudice and discrimination have proved disturbingly stubborn, and so we study these problems in chapter three. Moreover, the immigrant-host model tends to neglect the ethnic affiliations and group aspirations of the migrants and their descendants. The importance of these ethnic features suggests the need for careful ethnographic studies, and these are explored in chapter four. Finally, in chapter five, we consider those approaches which trace the main problems to the underlying tensions and structural strains of British society. The primary focus of the book is modern Britain, although the leading arguments are supported by necessary reference to historical and international evidence.

The greater part of this book was written by John Richardson, but it arose from a genuinely collaborative enterprise. We should like to express our gratitude to Michael Haralambos for his generous editorial advice, and to Ann Braddon, Phyllis Thomas and Pat Harris for their invaluable secretarial assistance.

Chapter One

Race and Sociology

This book is about the way sociologists have tried to come to terms with the nature and causes of those conflicts and problems that are termed 'race relations' problems. This book would not have been written if there was not a widespread recognition that there are indeed severe race relations *problems*. For some, of course, such problems are the fault of, or caused by, racial or ethnic minorities. For others the problems are caused by racists and by racism.

An important task for sociology is to assess the significance of various explanations, and at the outset it may be useful to distinguish five traditions or perspectives, in order to locate sociology's special contribution.

Perspectives on Race

(1) **The 'moral' approach.** In this view, the problems associated with 'race' are reducible to fundamental moral issues. Racism is attributed to outright human wickedness, or to common human failings such as selfishness and ignorance. The appropriate solution, then, lies in critical soul-searching, appealing to nobler moral values, and in affirming the dignity and worth of all members of the one human race. Rather predictably, social scientists tend to dismiss this moral approach as 'naïve' and hoplessly abstract, but it is certainly true that race relations present urgent moral choices, and this means that the banishment of moral considerations would be misguided. However, it is far more informative to locate moral issues within specific social and historical contexts. Why, for example, does racial goodwill vary between societies and within one society over time? What are the obstacles (e.g. financial interests, power relationships) which stand in the way of inter-racial harmony? By asking these sorts of questions, the

sociologist reaches beyond abstract moral debate towards a more socially informed examination of the particular types of environments and interests which shape moral choices.

(2) The 'biological' approach. At its simplest, this approach assumes that prejudice against 'out-groups' is a more or less natural instinct, determined by some genetic code which supposedly enhances survival chances (e.g. by favouring people of similar appearance, the survival chances of the 'selfish gene' are improved). Furthermore, the social disadvantages of ethnic minorities are portrayed as a direct reflection of their innate inferiority (e.g. the poor educational results and low status jobs of minority groups are explained not by prejudice nor discrimination nor cultural dislocation, but by their allegedly inferior IQ levels or by some biologically-based inability to develop sophisticated cultures). However, as we will argue later in this chapter, the sociologist can safely ignore these discredited and highly misleading views. It is the social meanings of biological differences which matter, not the biological differences in themselves.

(3) The 'psychological' approach. Rather than describing prejudice as an inborn mechanism triggered off by the mere sight of people of different physical appearance, psychologists are far more likely to resort to explanations in terms of learning experiences, personality quirks, and the general psychological processes involved in attitude formation. Thus, certain high-risk personalities (subjected to unfortunate socialisation) may be especially predisposed towards bigotry; or perhaps prejudice has more general currency among small groups exposed to recurrent psychological frustrations (e.g. the frustration-aggression model, in which cumulative psychological frustrations result in a fund of aggression which may be displaced on to some 'safe' scapegoat group). As for social disadvantage, this can be explained by the direct discriminatory practices of the prejudiced, or by the demoralisation and lowered self-esteem of the victims of racism. Some of these psychological arguments undoubtedly illuminate important areas and dimensions in race relations.

(4) The 'cultural' approach. This approach also tackles 'attitudes', but from a sociological orientation which makes few references to personalities or mental processes. Instead, emphasis is placed upon the dynamics of 'cultural' allegiances and traditions, and the main interest lies in the social origins, functions and consequences of these cultural phenomena. In this model, cultural racism has its roots in the dim colonial past, but the racist stereotypes developed during that period

are transmitted to succeeding generations as part of the general folk-lore, and it is by inculcating this cultural tradition that white people develop prejudices against blacks. Another, contemporary, version, explains racial friction as a form of 'ethnic conflict' sparked off by groups jealously guarding the integrity of their distinctive cultural identities. The 'ethnicity' approach, which we elaborate in Chapter 4, also allows that much racial disadvantage is not due to racialism pure and simple, but to wider cultural factors (lack of familiarity with British language and customs; voluntary segregation; continued ties with 'home' country).

(5) The 'structural' approach. This group of explanations traces the reasons for racism back to the major structural features and social processes of the dominant society. So the main source of racism is located not in the hearts and minds of people, nor in abstract cultural allegiances, but firmly in the principal structural arrangements of the society. If the social structure systematically generates sharp conflicts of material interests, or if it breeds cumulative social frustrations, then this is likely to fan the flames of racial prejudice (e.g. whites blame blacks for what in fact are structurally-created problems of unemploy-ment, housing shortages, and so on). Moreover, racial minorities in Britain generally have insufficient power to compete successfully in the economic and political struggle for scarce resources, and therefore they constitute a disadvantaged section of the population. In these sorts of ways, the basic social structure (the key institutions, patterned social networks, and especially the stratification system) crucially affects the nature of race relations and the life chances of racial minorities.

This brief review of the major perspectives available for explaining problems and issues of race relations helps to establish a distinctive sociological approach, but clearly these perspectives cannot be rigidly separated, and in the chapters which follow we will explore aspects of their differences and of their overlap.

A particular set of complications arise from the broad sweep of structural and cultural explanations – the major concern of the sociologist. Although all structural approaches rely on structural 'strains' and 'tensions' as a clue to understanding race relations, this shared emphasis still accommodates an interesting diversity of detailed arguments. Some indication of this diversity is provided by Taylor (1982), who usefully describes the many explanations which can be used to make sense of the 'race riots' (or 'urban riots', since they included white participants) which broke out in such inner-city areas as Brixton, St. Pauls and Toxteth in the early 1980s. The British riots represent a fertile testing-ground for structural explanations, and Taylor shows that nearly all literature on riots refers to structural factors, usually broken down into long-term 'preconditions' (such as unemployment and urban deprivation) and the more immediate 'precipitants' of conflict (such as police ineptitude or heavy-handedness). Nevertheless, this still leaves a bewildering variety of specific explanations, in terms of such things as system malfunctions, underclass revolt, internal colonialism, political marginalisation, 'pressure-cooker' theories of violence, failures of policy initiatives, ecological defence, and several other accounts. Taylor wisely contends that no single 'factor' can adequately explain the outbreak of violence and the eruption of frustrations, but he also suggests that theoretical frameworks are valuable in arranging the relevant factors and in drawing out the underlying processes. And, as in so many other branches of sociology, the dominant sociological frameworks for this task are the familiar ones of functionalism and conflict theory.

Functionalism – or the 'order' model – depicts society as a more or less integrated and cohesive system in which consensus is ensured by cooperative relationships between the various sub-systems and by a unifying set of common norms and values. Social elements persist because they fulfil some function which contributes towards the overall stability and survival of the system, and this system therefore serves the interests of all members of society. The system tends to rest in a state of equilibrium in which the tensions between the component sub-systems are reduced to a minimum, but occasionally this equilibrium is disrupted, and in this event self-regulating processes will come into play to restore stability. The functionalist model lends itself readily to the study of race relations, and the immigrant-host model described in Chapter 2 is perhaps the most striking example: here a stable host society is temporarily disturbed by the confusing arrival of new elements (the immigrants) who do not share the same values, and consensus is presumably restored by the 'healing' process of resocial-isation and long-term structural integration. Thus, Schermerhorn (1970) states that the systems approach dwells on:

> the functions the ethnic group performs for the entire system, viewing the ethnic group itself as a sub-system gradually fitting into the entire society by a series of adaptive adjustments regulated by the norms and values of its institutions that eventually become internalised by members of the ethnic groups involved.

However, the equilibrium-restoring mechanisms may prove

inadequate or slow, and these system failures will then result in blocked opportunity structures, unfulfilled aspirations, and social discontent. So the British riots can be accommodated within this framework, in spite of its bias towards 'consensus' rather than 'conflict'. Indeed, Mason (1981) indicates a close affinity between functionalism and the 'liberal reformist' assumptions of the famous Scarman Report (1981) on the riots:

> These assumptions include a view of social life in which individuals compete with one another for access to scarce resources, making, as they do so, rational decisions on the basis of more or less complete or accurate information. Racial disadvantage occurs when the normal opportunities for free competition are distorted by obstacles arising from economic misfortune (recession, urban decay), failures of policy (often resulting from inadequate information, misjudgement, and so on), or mischief-making (by pathologically prejudiced individuals and right-wing propagandists, aided again by inadequate information, education or training).

Drawing on this image of a basically sound society acting in the long-term interests of everyone, the Scarman Report regarded piecemeal reforms as the appropriate solution: the state was obliged to intervene to remove unfortunate social and economic obstacles which temporarily stood in the way of a fair deal for individual members of the ethnic minorities. The proposed reforms included employment and housing measures, the promotion of racial harmony, and steps to eradicate racial prejudice in the police force. However, it is the basic notion of a consensual, even-handed society whose problems can be remedied by *ad hoc* adjustments which most significantly differentiates the functionalist model from conflict approaches.

For the conflict theorist, either the favoured reforms do not go far enough, or they are unlikely to be implemented anyway because of the basic conflicts of interests between socio-economic groups. The conflict image of society is one of a continuous struggle between dominant and subordinate groups whose divergent sectional interests create divisive conflicts rather than stability and consensus. Society is based on systematic exploitation which benefits the powerful groups at the expense of others, but the dominant groups manage to maintain control by means of coercion and ideological manipulation. Still, the major strains and fierce tensions – or 'contradictions' – which are generated by an unfair and oppressive system are likely to encourage organised protest and opposition. Only a fundamental structural transformation and a significant shift in the balance of power will remove the distress and exploitation of the disadvantaged groups, and there is little prospect of ruling groups voluntarily passing legislation which will make deep inroads into their privileges or adversely affect their material interests.

The Delusion of Race

Whatever sociological framework or explanatory perspective is adopted, there is an unavoidable truth to face:

> As a way of categorising people, race is based upon a delusion, because popular ideas about racial classification lack scientific validity and are moulded by political pressures rather than by evidence from biology. (Banton and Harwood, 1975.)

In the aftermath of World War II which had seen the slaughter of the holocaust justified by a doctrine of racial superiority and the linked quest for racial purity to promote a master race for world order, the World's scientists unambiguously stated that there was no scientific basis for the belief that one race was superior to another:

> Current biological knowledge does not permit us to impute cultural achievements to differences in genetic potential. Differences in the achievements of different peoples should be attributed solely to their cultural history. The peoples of the world today appear to possess equal biological potentialities for attaining any level of civilization. (UNESCO, 1967.)

But as we all know, the delusion, and actions based on it, persist worldwide. In the field of race relations, W. I. Thomas's famous sociological dictum has immediate relevance: if people define a situation as real, it is real in its social consequences. Thus, if white people actually believe that blacks are congenitally inferior and irredeemably primitive, then this attitude constitutes their social reality, and it will influence their subsequent behaviour towards blacks. Likewise, if Rastafarians believe that all whites are corrupt plotters in a sinister 'Babylonian conspiracy', then this may well have far-reaching consequences in their dealings with white people. So social attitudes and constructions of 'race' are not just interesting curiosities: they form the medium of exchange in daily interaction between the groups concerned. We need to examine the roots of the delusion.

The Doctrine of Racial Superiority

Banton (1977) notes how various nineteenth century thinkers were impressed both by the rapid advances in biology and zoology and by the tremendous technological achievements of Western European powers. Consequently, they became fascinated with the prospect of constructing taxonomies (classifications) of human beings which introduced a link between racial attributes and moral and cultural superiority. These writers did not always agree on important details, and so competing taxonomies were canvassed and fiercely debated, but beneath this surface rivalry there existed a shared set of assumptions which Banton calls the 'theory of racial typology'. This entailed the following propositions:

(1) Variations in the physical appearance of peoples indicate distinctive racial 'types' of a fixed, permanent kind.
(2) These racial 'types' develop markedly different cultures, since culture is decisively influenced by biological status.
(3) It is possible, therefore, to acknowledge the superiority of Europeans in general, and 'Aryans' in particular.
(4) Friction between nations or different racial groups is 'natural' insofar as it springs ultimately from biological sources.

Although these assertions have now been discredited or modified out of all recognition – at least as far as respectable science is concerned – they nevertheless survive as lingering components of 'commonsense' views: in particular, the notion of races as more or less fixed, mutually exclusive groups arranged in some hierarchy of superiority. The unsupportable nature of the doctrine of racial superiority can be demonstrated, however, if we pursue two basic questions:

(1) What is a 'race'?
(2) What is the relationship between biology and culture?

What is a Race?

Biologists and botanists generally find it useful to construct taxonomies which identify and arrange different species and their related sub-groups. Just as it is possible to distinguish plants and animals in this way, so attempts were made from the nineteenth century on to classify human beings according to physical and biological criteria. Inevitably this enterprise threw up a number of fanciful and crankish ideas (including the dangerously misleading theory of racial typology), but gradually a firmer understanding developed. Thus, it became clear that all human beings belong to a single species, in the sense that the various 'members' are potentially capable of producing fertile offspring if they mate with each other. But the members differ noticeably in physical appearance, and so the term 'race' has been adopted to denote a recognisable sub-division of the species. UNESCO, for example, has used the term to refer to groups of humanity showing well-developed and primarily heritable physical differences from other groups. For convenience, then, various 'physical markers' have been employed to map the boundaries between one race and another. No single physical feature is sufficiently sensitive for this purpose, but normally the working assumption is made that certain 'clusters' of physical characteristics – hair type, skin colour, nasal shape, lip form, etc. – permit reasonable demarcation. This assumption lies behind the familiar distinction between Mongoloid, Negroid and Caucasoid races (see Table 1).

Table 1.   Conventional taxonomy of phenotypical differences

Racial Group	Eyes	Hair	Skin	Face	Main location
Mongoloid	Black 'slanted'	Black straight	Yellow-reddish brown	Flat, high cheekbones, sparse beard	S & E Asia, N & S America Pacific
Negroid	Brown	Black tightly curled	Dark brown-black	Broad nose, wide nostrils, thick lips, sparse beard	Sub-Saharan African
Caucasoid	Light blue to dark brown	Straight, wavy, curly, balding more common	White to dark brown	Narrow nose thin lips, more facial hair	Europe, M. East N. Africa, India

Clearly, this classification is very broad and sweeping, and so it does not totally succeed in avoiding awkward cases (e.g. are Bushmen and aboriginals part of the Negroid group, or do they constitute a separate race?). This type of problem has led to the construction of yet further sub-groups within each racial division. In the Caucasoid group, for example, the distinction between 'whites' and 'Asian Indians' is obvious enough. But there is also a division between various European groups (Nordic, Alpine and Mediterranean). Nevertheless, subsequent modifications of this basic schema have not resulted in acceptably tidy groupings, and so the classification still remains no more than suggestive. Moreover, it has become increasingly apparent that there are more informative means of distinguishing between human groupings, in terms of the altogether more reliable methods of modern genetics.

The technical details of genetics are not important here – suffice to say that each human body consists of many thousands of genes which incorporate chemical codes in complex permutations and which account for the unique character of individuals. Modern knowledge in genetics casts considerable doubts on the validity and utility of the older taxonomics based on physical appearance. The relationship between *genotype* – the underlying genetic patterning of individuals and groups – and *phenotype* – the difference and patterns of physical appearance – is extraordinarily complex. In particular, the following three aspects should be noted:

(1) The older notion of 'race' referred to a few broad groups, distinguished by selected phenotypical differences. This has been replaced by the more sophisticated and flexible concept of numerous 'gene pools' or 'populations', each marked out by a characteristic 'genetic profile'. Thus, even within a relatively small geographical area, local populations may differ in the frequencies of certain genes. The patterns of genetic traits are determined by various factors: climate, physical environment, diet, genetic mutations which affect adaptation, genetic drift (selective migration), geographical barriers (seas, mountains, deserts) and social influences (mating and breeding patterns, and political forces like apartheid).

(2) Modern genetics shifts us away from the notion of static, permanent 'types' towards a much more fluid conception of human groupings. These groups are seen as part of a general evolutionary process in which change is occurring all the time. Genetic mutation, breeding and inter-breeding patterns, and changing environmental circumstances make it improbable that the genetic profile of a group will remain constant.

(3) The notion of 'pure' race is misleading in the extreme. Firstly, there is considerable diversity within any group, since its members do not share exactly the same genes. But even more importantly, there is considerable continuity and overlap between groups. The basic under-lying human genotype (e.g. genes which determine that we have two legs, a prehensible thumb, etc.) suggests that the differences are less striking than the similarities. Moreover, the differences which do exist typically relate not to the presence or absence of certain genes, but rather to the *statistical* frequencies of those genes in the populations being compared.

Biology and Culture

The other leading assertion in the theory of racial typology concerns the alleged link between biology and culture. Proponents of the doctrine argued that there was a strong causal connection, so that the biological level set limits on the cultural achievements of 'inferior' races and at the same time encouraged the relatively unhampered progress of 'superior' races. Such arguments tended to be presented in confident fashion, as if they were the irresistible conclusions of sound scientific research. It does not take a great stretch of the imagination to appreciate the social and political attractions of such ideas in the nineteenth century. They proved a useful rallying point for the British nation in its efforts to forge and consolidate an Empire; they acted as an inspiration to further cultural achievement, and they simultaneously legitimised imperial ventures (e.g. the Empire was seen as a 'civilising' mission to help 'backward' peoples). In this respect, the theory of racial typology was not so much a neutral scientific statement, but rather an integral part of an over-arching ideology which played an important role in a situation of social and political conflict. And this ideology gained strength by appearing not simply as a case of special pleading or political intrigue but as based on solid scientific 'fact', and this is what the proponents of the theory of racial typology promised to provide.

The motives of those scientists must be separated from the issue of the consequences and social effects of their writings, including the ways in which politicians adopted and used their ideas. Banton is surely correct in insisting that genuine scientific errors were made, and that in the nineteenth century context these racial ideas had a certain surface plausibility. For example, Darwin's evolutionary theory seemed to reinforce the notion of a biologically-based hierarchy of human types with each race representing successive 'stages' in evolutionary advancement. And even today we still find tentative advocates of the core ideas enshrined in the theory of racial typology. Belief in racial superiority of sorts still prevails – in a much more guarded and sophisticated form – in those 'scientific' theories (e.g. sociobiology) which contend that apparent racial differences in intelligence and social behaviour are ultimately attributable to biological causes. However, the champions of this line of reasoning have not been conspicuously successful in establishing their case. We can now look briefly at some of the reasons for their lack of success:

(1) Firstly, it is extremely difficult to identify the precise links between the biological level and socio-cultural phenomena. Given the immense complexity of genetic processes, it is perhaps not surprising

that the supposed biological causes tend to be assumed rather than convincingly demonstrated. Most commonly, the writers concerned start from rather broad socio-cultural differences, then proceed to speculate on some underlying, as yet unspecified, biological mechanisms which are presumably responsible for these differences. Now, it would be foolish to suggest that biology has no bearing on socio-cultural behaviour, but, with the exception of some biological abnormalities which result in low intelligence or bizarre behaviour, we would normally expect the linkages to be remote and indirect. The whole task becomes much more perplexing when a racial dimension is included, because then we would expect the proponents to show that socio-cultural patterns neatly, or even nearly, coincide with the lines of biologically-defined races. No such correspondence is demonstrable.

(2) Powerful explanations of social phenomena can be offered without resorting to biological 'reductionism' (explaining events at one level by referring to a 'lower', presumably more basic, level). Indeed, sociology is based on a firm recognition of the 'autonomy' of the social level, on the necessity of dealing with social events in their own terms. Unlike animals, human beings are not so rigidly bound to inbuilt instincts or innate biological triggers; on the contrary, human survival and progress is enhanced if cultural flexibility prevails. So, while biology is obviously important (we would not be recognisably 'human', or even exist, without our biology), it sets only rather broad limits on cultural development. To this extent, then, human beings are 'freed' from biological destiny. A clear illustration of this is the way in which a given 'race' can create quite contrasting 'cultures' in different geographical locations; likewise, members of separate biological 'races' may contribute to the development of a single 'culture' in a particular society. Therefore the complex social, political and historical manifestations of 'race' demand study in their own right, rather than being dismissed in favour of deterministic biological 'programmes'.

(3) The notion of 'cultural superiority' is highly problematic. What are the yardsticks by which we assess the relative merits of different cultures? People tend to judge these matters from an 'ethnocentric' viewpoint which predisposes them to value the 'familiar' and to disparage other cultures. What lent racial doctrines a certain credibility was the impressive technological spurt of Western European nations in recent centuries, but claims of 'progress' appear less convincing when we consider the subsequent problems of industrial pollution, personal alienation, and the possibility of nuclear warfare. The African pygmy or Mongolian herdsman is arguably in a more 'harmonious' relationship with his physical and human environment than is the

urban inhabitant of London or New York. However, the main point is that cultural achievements do not thereby demonstrate some 'innate' or permanent superiority, as a glance at history quickly reveals. For example, ethnocentric white Europeans tend to overlook proud African civilisations of the past, such as the Songhai, Ashanti and Zimbabwe empires, at a time when Europe was in the 'Dark Ages'. Also, Goldthorpe (1975) argues that, in 1600, an impartial observer would probably have rated China as the most 'developed' nation, with India and Arabia vying for second place. Plainly, the history of racial achievement resembles a see-saw, so it offers no compelling evidence for undisputed racial superiority.

The Intelligence Controversy

In spite of these telling points, the thorny debate about racial superiority gained fresh impetus in the late 1960s, and this time it focussed squarely on the issue of intelligence. In the United States the key figure was Jensen (1969), who argued that compensatory 'environmental' programmes to boost educational performance had failed dismally thereby suggesting the overriding importance of heredity. Meanwhile in Britain, Eysenck (1971) concluded that the research findings of psychometrics (the testing and measuring of mental capacities) indicated distinct racial differences in intellectual abilities. For example, in the USA the average IQ score of black groups lagged about fifteen points behind the average score of equivalent white groups. Although the 'hereditarian' views of Eysenck and Jensen soon came under fierce attack, opponents tended to be dismissed as rather utopian idealists whose liberal values prevented them from recognising the 'objective' evidence of 'hard-headed' scientists. However, the irony is that the most authoritative criticism emerged from within the scientific community itself, and it is the scientific credentials of the hereditarian arguments which have been shown to be suspect. The numerous methodological deficiences – poor research design, circumstantial evidence, tests of dubious validity, etc. – have been rehearsed elsewhere (Kamin, 1981) and need not detain us here. Still, it is important to note that the case of 'intelligence' definitely does *not* lend belated support to the doctrine of racial superiority.

First of all, it is perfectly obvious that members of a given 'race' are not confined to a narrow IQ band. Whatever IQ tests measure – and this is a matter of some controversy – it is nonetheless evident that members typically spread over the whole range of possible scores. Therefore the scores of different 'races' exhibit considerable overlap, and so the debate only concerns group averages (no one suggests that all – or even most – members of one group are superior to, or inferior to, the members of another group). Moreover, the weakness in crude hereditarian arguments is most clearly exposed when we examine the alleged link between biology and IQ. The debate between 'nature' and 'nurture' is perennial because, while everyone recognises the influence of heredity and of environment, there are no reliable means of assessing their *relative* contributions. Despite this major obstacle, the indefensible hereditarian argument over-confidently asserts that IQ tests are a valid measure of a 'fixed', 'intrinsic' ability which is largely genetically determined; and that this genetic determination suggests relatively unchangeable IQ differences between races. But already we have seen that 'races' themselves are not unchanging, and we have also noted that the IQ differences are of a small magnitude. Furthermore, environmental influences just cannot be assigned the minor role of simply 'topping-up' a given genetic potential. Even the most convinced environmentalists accept some underlying genetic contribution to intelligence, but they insist that intellectual development springs from the unique, dynamic *interaction* of genes and environment. Consequently, there is little way of knowing how a given individual or group would have turned out if environmental circumstances had been otherwise. John Rex (1973) has aptly pointed to the contrasts in the different environments of white and black in America and suggests that there can be no true comparison without an experiment in which:

> The peoples of Africa conquer, capture and enslave some millions of European and American whites, under conditions in which a very large proportion of the white population dies, in which the white culture is systematically destroyed, and in which, finally, a group of emancipated whites in 'good neighbourhoods' are then compared to their negro masters... the differences in the history of negroes and whites are a factor of immense significance, and... any statistical reasoning which leaves them out can reach no conclusions of any value whatever.

The Social Construction of Race

We have shown that, scientifically speaking, *race* (in the sense of 'gene pools') refers to clusters of biological characteristics which are changeable rather than unalterably fixed and which relate to gradually altering gene frequencies among diverse human groups rather than to clearly identifiable basic human types. We have shown, too, how the idea that there is a strong causal chain between the biological level and the sphere of socio-cultural behaviour is untenable. Science cannot give support to the idea that social characteristics and cultural forms are biologically programmed either in essential detail or in broad general sweep. There is no demonstrable genetic basis for cannibalism or for Christianity, for rising divorce rates, shifts in fashion of clothes or music, or for racial hatred. Social customs and patterns of behaviour are not pre-determined by rigid laws of nature incorporated in the genes, but emerge in the course of social interaction. Social reality is *socially* constructed.

So the sociologist can safely leave biology aside and concentrate on how race is socially constructed. Once people choose to attribute variable social meanings to physical differences and behave as if biology *did* fix attributes and abilities, then *that* becomes part of social reality. What people make of physical differences, the everyday or commonsense notions which influence them, constitutes the social meaning of race. The distinction that Banton (1974) draws between 'analytical' and 'folk' concepts of race is useful. Race, in the scientific or analytical sense, has limited relevance as a rough indicator of clusters of gene pools. But in this book we are primarily concerned with the 'folk' concept, the everyday attitudes regarding racial differences.

Far from being 'natural' or 'instinctive', these social attitudes to race tend to vary according to time and place. In some societies, at certain times, people are found to attach little weight to racial differences, while in other contexts we might find intense hostility and pronounced patterns of racial 'exclusion' and 'inclusion'.

But a sociology of race reaches beyond the description of relevant belief systems towards a search for the social factors which shape and condition those beliefs. It is not satisfactory to accept cultural beliefs as 'given' or simply 'there', as if they were plucked arbitrarily from thin air. Rather, we would expect that a society's 'culture' (its network of attitudes, values, meanings and ideologies) is connected in intimate ways which its 'structure' (the pattern of social institutions, productive arrangements and power relationships). The distinctive emphasis on the 'social construction of reality' allows that human beings have a genuinely active role in striving to create and sustain meanings and in generally asserting themselves in the world. Nevertheless, this creative work takes place within particular historical and structural contexts which tend to limit human choices and make certain types of cultural response and behaviour more likely than others. It is in this dynamic interplay – people creating 'social reality', and this social reality acting back on people – that the social construction of race can be located.

Therefore, if hostile racist attitudes are widespread in a society, then we might expect to discover something in the history or social structure of that society which predisposes people towards these attitudes. Perhaps internal conflict is so rife that it creates the need for racial 'scapegoats' to ease social tensions; or perhaps powerful groups are manipulating racial prejudices in order to weaken and exploit racial minorities for the purpose of economic gain. As Schermerhorn (1970) remarks, 'prejudice is a product of situations, historical situations, economic situations, political situations; it is not a little demon that emerges in people simply because they are depraved'. Of course, racial attitudes are not simply a direct automatic reflection of social situations: to a certain extent they gain momentum of their own, interacting with other cultural elements (e.g. political and religious ideologies) and acting back on and changing the structural reality itself. So culture and structure interact in complex and shifting ways, and it is unrealistic to expect an absolutely straightforward match between particular types of racial belief systems and distinctive types of social structure. Nevertheless, the social structure provides valuable clues to the source and consequences of racial hostility.

The sociology of race, then, entails the study of social consciousness, of inter-group behaviour and of social structure. By focussing attention on three sociologists' treatment of race in contemporary Britain we can discover the key elements in the search for a distinctive sociology of race: John Rex, a noted Weberian; Robert Miles, writing from a Marxist standpoint; and Michael Banton, writing from a more eclectic standpoint rooted in social anthropology and role theory, and closer perhaps to the British empirical tradition in social sciences.

John Rex's work represents the most developed attempt to demarcate a special domain of race relations entailing a distinct set of social phenomena. A persistent theme in his writings is the insistence that 'race' must be taken seriously as a social issue and as a sociological concept. Of course, Rex is fully aware that the social meanings of race contain numerous errors and falsehoods, but what matters is the human actor's point of view, and he recognises the ways in which subjective understandings of race translate themselves into objective consequences. However, he is at pains to stress that race problems are not solely a matter of mistaken ideas or false consciousness, and he does not believe that these problems will simply vanish if the errors are challenged. Alongside the subjective definitions, then, due attention must be paid to the underlying social structures which help create and sustain racial belief systems and racial tensions.

Rex's various studies underline his concern to develop a rigorous, theoretically informed definition of the appropriate subject matter for a sociology of race. He sees three necessary (but not sufficient) conditions for a fully fledged race relations situation, structure or problem. These are:

(1) A social situation in which at least two groups co-exist in a context of inequality and conflict.

(2) The boundaries between the groups are such that group categorization is on an ascriptive basis which limits movement between groups.

(3) The availability of *deterministic* belief systems which draw a causal link between group membership and social and cultural achievements, and in so doing provide a justification for discrimination. These belief systems may be systematic biological or theological doctrines, or may be current as 'folklore', 'proverbs', or 'superstition'. (Rex 1970.)

Each of these elements has a certain measure of independence, and each deserves special attention, but Rex is primarily interested in their interrelations. For Rex, the main task of a sociology of race is the detailed analysis, along comparative and historical lines, of the major types of race relations situations.

The sociological influence of Max Weber is very apparent in Rex's writing – his concern to focus on social meanings, an action frame of reference, his concern for comparative and historical work, but essentially his presentation of social order and structure arising out of *diverse* intergroup conflicts, among which those relating to production and the organising of the economy are important, but not necessarily paramount. Within that sociological framework there is room for a distinct sociology of race.

For Robert Miles, such an enterprise is quite misguided because 'race relations' is not a legitimate sphere of study. If race has that highly limited scientific validity to which we referred earlier, then for sociologists to treat it as an analytic concept with explanatory significance is a nonsense – and a dangerous nonsense, because it becomes part of the process whereby the error of race persists (Miles 1982).

Just as stratification theorists develop their own analytical concepts rather than relying on 'folk views' of class, so, Miles suggests, sociologists should abandon concepts like 'race' or 'race relations' and rely instead on more valid categories and concepts. Otherwise, they merely introduce misleading commonsense discourse into academic thought, and in so doing seem to bestow credibility on those flawed commonsense views. Also, the retention of terms like 'race' or 'race relations' seems to suggest that 'race' has some independent force: race becomes a causal factor in its own right, something with 'real', 'objective' status which influences and determines social events. Against this, Miles seeks to locate the delusion within an essentially Marxist framework where the organisation of production and its attendant class relations in capitalist society shape intergroup conflicts, including 'race' conflicts (and in Miles's work 'race' is always in inverted commas). Explanations of 'race and racism' are to be sought in the exploited role of migrant labour in the economies of advanced capitalist countries. It is the distinctive economic structure which shapes the social reality of intergroup conflicts, the violence and discrimination and politics of hate (the social significance of which Miles in no way seeks to deny). Miles recognises the existence of a set of beliefs about the inferiority of black races, and 'racism' is the important concept he uses to characterise an ideology with potent implications for class struggle. Another author who writes from a Marxist standpoint is Stuart Hall, and he has written of racism as a prism which misrepresents the pattern of class relations as race relations (Hall, 1978). Miles would seem to share this view, whilst also acknowledging as real what he calls a 'racialised fraction' of social class, due to the tendency for black migrant workers in Britain to be concentrated in certain kinds of work positions outside the mainstream of secure unionised and good status positions. The task for sociology, in Miles's view, is to reveal, behind the distortions and delusions, the class structure of society.

A much more provisional approach is favoured by Michael Banton (1977), who simply proposes that the sociology of race relations is distinguished by its 'tradition of enquiry'. Such a tradition incorporates sets of ideas of how to go about the task, what topics to investigate, and what methods to use. According to this recommendation, then, there is no need to erect rigid boundaries or impose authoritative definitions in advance – instead, the area of study is roughly mapped by the familiar preoccupations, of self-designated 'race relations' specialists. One such preoccupation, quite obviously, is the 'social construction of race', and another is the notion of 'inclusion-exclusion boundaries' between socially-defined racial groups. But the tradition of enquiry will gradually alter as knowledge progresses and new interests are added. Moreover, Banton does not wish to represent 'race relations' as a special ghetto requiring unique concepts or exclusive theories, and so he invites the sociologist of race to ransack adjoining sociological areas (minorities, stratification, culture, deviancy, religion, etc.). The attractiveness of Banton's conceptualisation lies in its flexibility and tolerance. Any insistence on a strict definition of the field runs the danger of raising unproductive controversies and prematurely closing off potentially valuable areas of exploration. But Banton's approach makes few dogmatic assumptions, and it allows us to leave open the question of whether 'objective' or 'subjective' factors are fundamental, and whether 'race' or 'class' is the main determinant of social action.

Each of these authors, we should note, root their analysis and argument in detailed study of social relations in contemporary Britain, and each contribution is distinctive. Where they differ is perhaps not so much over whether there is a 'field' there which deserves attention, but over their more specific theoretical allegiances. But it is out of such diversity and debate that the sociological understanding of race and race relations emerges.

Chapter Two

Britain: Hosts and Immigrants

Our main task in this chapter is to note some special features of the arrival into Britain of significant numbers of 'coloured' immigrants whose presence – or more correctly *the response* to whose presence – has prompted the current race relations situation. The recent immigration and its response created what became termed a 'numbers game' as commentators vied with each other for the most accurate claims and counter claims of the past, present and future size of the immigrant population. It proved a game of considerable complexity which generated much heat but little light – not least because of the difficulty of agreeing who were 'the immigrants'.

It needs only the briefest of surveys of British history to emphasise how our island history is punctuated with arrivals of peoples of diverse sorts. The early Roman invaders encountered a mixed population of Britons, Picts and Celts, and when the Romans finally withdrew from these shores in 410 A.D. the succeeding centuries witnessed a series of forays and scattered settlements by varied groups of Angles, Saxons, Jutes, Danes and Vikings. This diversity was significantly enhanced by the arrival of the Normans, who not only had a profound influence on the laws, language and manners of the country, but also established more active lines of contact and exchange with the rest of Europe. The subsequent development of trade links and political alliances helped ensure thereafter that the 'insularity' of the island was always partial and relative.

Among the varied groups of immigrants from about the seventeenth century, it was the Irish whose labour power contributed hugely to the industrial revolution. The still current term 'Navvy' derives from the gangs of workers, largely Irish, who laboured to construct the Navigation canals and later the railways. Irish migration swelled even more when the harrowing potato famines of the mid-1840s led to a mass exodus. The 1851 census estimated that there were at least half a million Irish-born living in the ports and industrial areas of England, Scotland and Wales. Although the pace of Irish immigration slackened somewhat after this period, it continued at a steady level and even accelerated in the twentieth century.

Another important immigrant group to be considered are the Jews, who first arrived in England in the wake of the Norman conquest. Like the Irish, they were met by a great deal of initial hostility, and indeed in 1290 they were expelled from England, only to reappear about 400 years later when Cromwell allowed them back. From that date there was a relatively modest growth in the Jewish population in Britain until a sudden upsurge in the latter years of the nineteenth century when there was a rush of Jewish refugees fleeing persecution and pogroms in Russia and Eastern Europe. Although the United States was the final port of destination for many of them, a considerable number settled in London, and by the time of the First World War the total Jewish community was estimated at around a quarter of a million.

Contrary to popular belief, the presence of coloured people in Britain is not a recent phenomenon. Fryer (1984) documents how blacks (Africans and Asians) have been living in Britain for close on 500 years – longer, if we include those who accompanied the Roman armies – and they have been born in Britain since about 1505. Advances in ship-building and in navigational skills obviously facilitated long-distance population transfers, but black migration must also be located against the backcloth of the steady growth of world trade and the spectacular expansion of the British Empire. As Hall (1978) observes, Britain's relations with the peoples of the Caribbean and the Indian sub-continent did not begin in the post-war period: for many centuries the 'imperialist chain' has indissolubly linked the fate of the peasants and workers in the colonies to the fortunes and actions of the people on the British mainland. In India, for example, we can trace the tentative establishment of British trading posts in the early seventeenth century, the haphazard and sometimes violent expansion of control in the eighteenth century, and the final consolidation of British rule in the nineteenth century, when India became the 'jewel in the crown' of the Victorian Empire. The history of the British Raj certainly contains episodes of violence and conflict, but these were undoubtedly surpassed by the sheer brutality of the slave trade and the establishment of sugar plantations in the West Indies. The British did not 'invent' the slave trade – the Portuguese were the first to export Negro slaves from the West African coast, and there was a previous history of slaving on the

African continent – but they increasingly played a prominent role. There were early slave trading ventures by English seafarers in the sixteenth century, but it was the creation of sugar plantations in the West Indies from the mid-seventeenth century on which resulted in a massive increase in slave transportation. Black Africans became human 'commodities' to be exchanged within the 'triangular trade route': British merchants shipped manufactured goods which were exchanged for black slaves on the West Coast of Africa; these slaves were then transported to the West Indies where they would be sold, and the money used to purchase sugar (or sometimes tobacco, cotton or molasses) which was resold in Britain. Great profits were made for British merchants and plantation owners, but at the cost of immense human misery and a heavy toll in human lives.

Amidst the hustle and bustle of trade and empire, black communities began to develop in Britain itself and in the mid-eighteenth century it was estimated that perhaps 20,000 black people were settled in Britain. But the black population did not grow: repatriation was talked about and promoted; trade patterns tended to maintain a demand for black labour in the colonies; and if black manservants were a status symbol of the fashionable wealthy, black families were very few. It was the later rise in tempo of the industrialising process which brought more ships to British ports and the gradual development of coloured settlements. The Indian trade brought Sikh pedlars of cloth to ply their special trade; and a small elite of Indian businessmen and administrators came for training or education for themselves or their sons. If the elite get caricatured in the upper class novels and games of the Victorian and Edwardian periods, the experience of the others was frequently far from 'cricket'. Race riots were a feature of a number of poor towns in the immediate aftermath of World War 1 as concern about unemployment rose.

It was the Second World War which caused a significant increase in the numbers of coloured immigrants – the thousands of Indian and West Indian troops whose war service brought them through Britain to the various fronts in which they played so notable a part. After demobilization in 1945 it was estimated that some 10,000 blacks were resident in Britain. But it was the following years which were to witness the largest increases in Britain's coloured population.

New Commonwealth Migration

The 'Old Commonwealth' is a term which refers to the long-established dominions or self-governing territories of the British

Commonwealth – Australia, Canada, New Zealand – which have a largely, but not exclusively, white population. Those ex-colonies which gained formal independence during the period since the Second World War are generally described as the 'New Commonwealth' (or, after Pakistan's secession from the Commonwealth in 1973, as the 'New Commonwealth and Pakistan'). It is these New Commonwealth countries which have provided the bulk of 'coloured' immigrants to Britain in the post-war period. Although the black presence in Britain has a long history, the scale of new Commonwealth migration eclipses earlier settlements in size and significance, and some familiarity with the contours of this migration is necessary for a full understanding of race relations in modern Britain.

The original reasons for migration obviously vary according to the groups and individuals concerned. Some of these 'sending' areas already had a tradition of migration (there was a well-trodden path between the West Indian islands and the United States and Canada; the Sikhs from the Punjab had soldiered round the world; and East African Asians had uprooted themselves from the Gujerat and Punjab areas of India in the 1920s and 1930s). So in some respects the migration to Britain fitted into a longer tradition of mobility. But in addition there were new incentives which appeared. For example, the 1947 partition of India (into India, and West and East Pakistan) led to millions of people crossing the newly-created borders because of fears for their safety, and the ensuing upheaval provoked further migration. Political conflict was also a powerful impetus to migration much later, around the 1970s, when the 'Africanisation' polices in Kenya, Uganda and Malawi placed increasing restrictions on the rights of Asian groups in those countries. But a constant spur to migration during the period under review was undoubtedly the desire for economic betterment. Whether it was the chronic unemployment or poverty of the West Indies, or the increasing population pressure on the land in India, the economic conditions of the sending countries compared unfavourably with the opportunities created in post-war Britain. Indeed, post-war Britain suffered an acute labour shortage, and although it attempted to fill the gap with European workers, there were still labour vacancies in many industries. As living standards in Britain steadily improved, the native population were reluctant to fill unpopular jobs in heavy or dirty industries (foundries, factories), low-paid jobs (textiles, manual jobs in National Health Service), and jobs which required regular shift work (transport, services). So, although migrants were also recruited to higher-status vacancies (doctors, nurses), they could be regarded largely as a low-level 'replacement population' which ensured the viability of essential services and industries. This responsiveness to labour needs determined that the post-war migrants were largely re-located in the industrial and growth areas of the South East and the major conurbations of the Midlands, Yorkshire and Greater Manchester, but considerable numbers gravitated to the old 'Empire' ports like Glasgow and Bristol.

The first main 'coloured group' to come to Britain in the post-war period were West Indians. There are great distances and cultural differences between the various West Indian islands, and island affiliations have been perpetuated in Britain in terms of geographical settlement and social relationships. The great majority of West Indian migrants originate from Jamaica, but Barbados, St. Kitts and other smaller islands are also represented. The trickle of migrants started in the late 1940s, and the main period of migration was the 1950s and early 1960s, after which it consisted mainly of dependents of the 'primary' settlers. The sex ratio among West Indian migrants has always tended to be rather evenly balanced, unlike the pattern among Asian migrants.

Migrants from the Asian sub-continent started rather later, in the 1950s, and the usual pattern was for men to act as the pioneers. A considerable number of Asian migrants had no firm plans to settle permanently in Britain, preferring to keep their options open, but gradually throughout the 1960s and 1970s the men were joined by wives and dependents (although the Pakistani community in Britain still has a preponderance of males). A particular feature of the Asian pattern was the phenomenon of 'chain migration' whereby a local village or kin group would routinely sponsor a series of migrants who either replaced or joined earlier migrants. This chain migration did not apply, of course, to the later Asian refugees from East Africa, who tended to arrive as complete families, and for whom there was little prospect of a return to Africa. These East African Asians, on the whole, were more prosperous and better-educated than their counterparts from the Indian sub-continent, although the African governments dispossessed many of them of their wealth and valuables before leaving the country. The East African Asians usually had a better command of the English language, but in many other cultural and religious respects they resembled the groups from the sub-continent. Most Asian migrants originate (directly, or via East Africa) from certain specific localities: the Punjab areas of India and Pakistan; the Gujerat region of India; the Sylhet area of Bangladesh (formerly East Pakistan); and the Mirpur and Kashmir regions of Pakistan. There are important cultural and linguistic differences between these areas, and of course there are major religious groups which can be identified. Most Pakistani and Bangladeshi migrants are Muslims (the largest religious group among Asians in Britain); and although there are also Muslims among the 'Indian' groups, Indians tend to be either Hindus or Sikhs (a group which broke away from the caste system of Hinduism, and which is recognisable by distinctive turbans for men). Therefore, just as there is a pattern of island groupings among 'West Indians' in Britian, so we have to recognise the varied religious, cultural and linguistic affiliations of the 'Asian' population.

As we suggested above, New Commonwealth migration played a valuable role in helping solve the post-war labour shortage in Britain, and some hard-pressed industries and employers even took the step of recruiting directly in those overseas countries. Thus, the National Health Service, London Transport, and various textiles and foundry companies either appointed local recruiting agents or advertised widely in the New Commonwealth countries. However, only a minority of the migrants were recruited directly in this manner, and for the most part the migration process was unregulated and unplanned. But this was to change in the 1960s when increasingly restrictive legislation was passed which curtailed rights of entry. Layton-Henry (1984) notes that post-war New Commonwealth migration had neither been widely anticipated nor welcomed by key policy-makers and politicians, but in spite of public disquiet little was done about it. Then, in the early 1960s the Conservative Party changed its policy on immigration. Layton-Henry suggests various reasons for this: the Conservatives felt that racial tension could be avoided only if controls were introduced; there was grass-roots pressure for restrictions from local constituency associations: it was no longer felt that the numbers were so small as to make restriction unnecessary; Britain's application for EEC membership weakened commitment to 'Commonwealth'; and there was a strong feeling that controls would be electorally popular. Consequently, the 1962 Commonwealth Immigration Act was passed, marking a decisive shift in the rights of Commonwealth citizens. Although it is true that 'aliens' have always been subject to vetting procedures, the notion of Commonwealth membership had seemed to secure a general right of entry. Even when independent Commonwealth countries such as Canada started introducing their own 'citizenship', this entailed no basic departure, and the 1948 British Nationality Act had guaranteed the rights of entry to Britain for every 'subject' or person born within the Empire and Commonwealth. But now, in the 1962 Act, this principle was undermined as controls were introduced: Commonwealth citizens without a passport issued in Britain were subject to an employment voucher system, and the numbers of these vouchers was limited. Moreover, the succeeding years were to witness a further tightening of entry controls. In 1968 a Labour Government passed the Commonwealth Immigrants Act, a panic measure to prevent a feared influx of Kenyan Asians expelled from that land. Although these Kenyan Asians had United Kingdom passports, the unprecedented step was taken of denying them entry as of right, unless certain strict requirements were met (e.g. if they had been born in Britain, or had a very close connection in some specified way). This 'close connection' idea was perpetuated and extended in the controversial 'patrials' clause enshrined in the 1971 Immigration Act. By restricting entry rights to 'patrials' (those born in Britain, or with a parent or grandparent born here, or adopted or naturalised in this country), this Act put a virtual end to all new 'coloured' immigration: most New Commonwealth migrants thereafter have entered under much the same controlled conditions as 'aliens', or else they have been dependents of already established primary settlers. Although a new British Nationality Act was passed in 1981, this was essentially a 'tidying-up' exercise (with several controversial elements) and the 1971 Act remains the working basis of present law.

Immigration laws are a highly complicated matter, and there are various loopholes, exemption clauses, and provisions for discretionary procedures and appeals. Sometimes the guidelines have been interpreted in a benevolent and liberal fashion – for example, large numbers of Kenyan Asians were eventually allowed to enter the country, in spite of the 1968 Act. However, a reasonable case can be made that the laws have been racist in their assumptions and intentions, and the main concern apparently has been to reduce *coloured* immigration while leaving white immigration relatively unrestricted. The 1971 Act, for example, actually made entry easier for many citizens of Old Commonwealth countries who had previously been subject to the voucher system, and the patrials clause seems a thinly disguised attempt to distinguish between white and black migrants. Moore (1975) has been especially critical of the laws, which he regards as flagrantly racist both in their basic conditions and in the discretionary practices which have accompanied them (e.g. applicants being callously treated by Embassy officials and immigration officers). In Moore's opinion, immigration laws involve a pernicious 'numbers game' which stigmatises blacks by defining them as a 'problem' whose numbers must be limited. Far from improving race relations, they reduce the security of those already settled (will their dependents be allowed in?, will there be moves to repatriation?), and encourage racist

groups to make even greater demands. The passage of anti-
discrimination legislation (e.g. the Race Relations Act of 1965, 1968
and 1971) therefore does not remove the damage done by immigration
laws which brand coloured migrants as undesirable intruders.

The Numbers Game

Moore's suspicions about the 'numbers game' are shared by many
commentators. Much of the politics of race has assumed that there is a
tolerable number, beyond which some new set of difficulties inevitably
develops: limit the numbers, send some home, and the problem
recedes.

However, the 'numbers game' was played without reliable figures on
the size of the coloured population. There was a tendency for many
whites to wildly exaggerate its size, fearing they would be swamped by a
massive influx of immigrants. Also, in the increasingly hostile world of

Table 2.   Ethnic Composition 1981

Ethnic Group	No. '000	%
White – born in Britain	48,335	90.0
White – born in Irish Republic	924	2.0
White – born in New Commonwealth Countries	446	1.0
White – born in Rest of the World or unstated or not known country	1,209	2.0
White sub-total	50,915	95.0
West Indian/Guyanese – Carribean born	463	0.90
– UK born	40	0.07
– born elsewhere	15	0.03
West Indian sub-total	519	1.0
Indian/Pakistan/Bangladesh – born there	831	1.54
– African born	164	0.35
– UK born	20	0.04
– born elsewhere	38	0.07
'Asian' sub-total	1,054	2.0
Other (including African, Arab and Chinese) – born abroad	327	0.52
– UK born	42	0.07
'Other' sub-total	369	0.6
Mixed ethnic origin – born abroad	135	0.25
– UK born	99	0.15
'Mixed' sub-total	234	0.4
Ethnic group not stated	608	1.0
All Ethnic groups	53,697	100

(Reproduced with the permission of the Controller of Her Majesty's Stationery Office) racial politics, minorities were worried about the use to which data on their numbers might be put. Such data are necessary, however, in order to establish whether coloured people are receiving a fair deal in such fields as education, jobs and housing. By the late 1970s, more reliable data on the ethnic composition of Britain began to emerge.

The 1981 Census did not include any special 'ethnic' question but it did ask respondents about birthplace. This census data shows that only about 3 out of every 100 households is headed by someone born in a New Commonwealth country (*Social Trends*, 1984). A more informative source is the *Labour Force Survey* based on data gained by interviewing a nationally and regionally representative sample of heads of households. The 1981 survey asked respondents to select the ethnic group to which they considered they, and the members of their household, belonged. *Social Trends* (1983) summarises this data as shown in Table 2.

This table reveals some interesting details. The first thing to note is the modest size of the non-British born and of the non-white population. Secondly, perhaps, is the evidence that coloured immigrants from the New Commonwealth and their families are outnumbered by families whose heads were born in other countries in Europe or elsewhere – by no means are all 'immigrants' 'coloured'. Thirdly, the tables bring out the *diversity* of the non-British born.

Ballard, in a recent article based on more detailed analysis of census data stresses that:

> Each of these groups has very different demographic characteristics. The Caribbeans, for instance, have the strongest local roots. Exactly half are now British born while at the other extreme only a quarter of the Bangladeshis are British in that sense. But the 1981 census shows, just as did all previous ones, that non-European immigrants are outnumbered by Europeans. The categories 'immigrant' and 'non-European' are in no sense synonymous, whatever popular usage may assume.
>
> Indeed, now that the minorities are an integral part of British society, a preoccupation with immigration is largely irrelevant. Attention is much more appropriately focussed on the minorities' local characteristics, and on their difference from or similarities with the remainder of the population. (Ballard, 1983.)

He goes on to emphasise the quite different age structures of the different groups and their differences from the age structure of the total population:

If you look at these figures overall, what do they tell you about Britain's minority populations? Most strikingly – that we can expect a steady process of growth in the coming years, regardless of any attempt to tighten yet further the screws of immigration control. That growth will occur for two reasons. As the population ages, so the number of people in the more elderly (and at present, rather empty) age slots will increase. Then there is the high birthrate in certain sections of the minority population, especially among Pakistanis and Bangladeshis. As long as this continues, it will fuel growth.

But even here we must retain a due sense of proportion. Estimates for the year 2000 do not anticipate that the population descended from the New Commonwealth migration of the '60s and '70s will then comprise more than 6 per cent of the population. Finally, it should be remembered that Britain exports population as well as importing migrants. In fact, over the last twenty or thirty years we more typically lose population through net migration (so much for fears of becoming overcrowded!). And by no means all of the emigrants from these isles are white; in fact, in some years we have lost more migrants to the West Indies than we have gained. In 1980, Britain accepted 30,000 migrants from the New Commonwealth (mostly dependants of previously settled kin folk) but exported 15,000 in return.

The Immigrant-Host Model

The steady flow of New Commonwealth migrants into post-war Britain sparked off numerous public controversies and media debates about where it was all heading. The British people, it was claimed, were troubled and uneasy at the prospect of fresh waves of migrants introducing 'alien' cultures, competing with the native population for jobs, and imposing heavy burdens on the social services. More liberal commentators, on the other hand, voiced anxieties about the welfare of the migrants themselves, and it was feared that racial prejudice would damage their morale and limit their social and economic opportunities. In the debates that emerged in the 1950s and 1960s, politicians and policy-makers, social scientists and journalists struggled to understand the key issues and predict the likely outcome. Different positions were adopted, ranging from outright hostility to the newcomers through to an enthusiastic welcome for their cultural and economic contributions, but it is possible to argue that there was a particular 'model' or framework of assumptions which tended to dominate the debates. In social science circles this was referred to as the *'immigrant-host'* model, but it is important to remember that the same sets of assumptions appeared in more 'popular' form, in the pages of newspapers and in general political discussion. The social science groundwork for the immigrant-host model had been performed earlier in the century by Robert Park (1950), a leading figure in the inter-war 'Chicago school' of sociologists. Park often resorted to analogies between 'social' and 'biological' phenomena, and he sometimes explained racial antipathy as a more or less spontaneous expression of deep-seated 'instincts'. Nevertheless, as a pioneer of 'social interactionism', Park also laid great stress on social relationships and social processes, and he is some-times credited as the first writer to set out theoretical guidelines for a sociology of race relations. So, in spite of certain inconsistencies and omissions in his own wide-ranging writings, he undoubtedly inspired interest in the sociology of race generally, and more specifically in the 'immigrant-host' model. This model has been developed in various ways since Park's time, and it has served as the guiding framework for some interesting field studies. But it is probably more accurate to regard it as a loose collection of assumptions rather than a rigorously-detailed and systematic explanatory theory. The model contains a general image of the nature of society, a statement about the most important features and problems of migration processes, and some suggestions about the likely direction of change. The leading assumptions of the model can now be outlined:

(a) The 'immigrants' entering the host society are portrayed first and foremost as 'strangers' who bring with them a quite different, and usually inappropriate, cultural tradition. It is this 'strangeness', rather than their race or colour, which constitutes the major impediment to their social acceptability and economic success. They may, for example, lack the necessary 'urban' or 'industrial' skills, and their sheer unfamiliarity with the customs and cultural demands of the host society places them at a considerable disadvantage.

(b) The 'hosts', typically, are depicted as confused, hesitant and insecure (Glass, 1960). Lacking detailed information about the newcomers' ways and habits, they respond in ambiguous fashion to the presence of the migrants, reacting at certain times in a hostile manner and yet at other times displaying commendable hospitality and tolerance. Apprehension is far more common than straight-forward prejudice.

(c) The immigrant-host model embraces an 'order' or 'consensus' image of society, in which the host society is described as basically stable and orderly and characterised by an ultimate consensus of values. There are no fundamental conflicts of interests which divide the population, and the host culture is reasonably homogeneous.

(d) The 'cultural' or 'value' consensus of the host society is temporarily disturbed by the entry of the migrants which creates a problem of disorganisation or dis-equilibrium. In the resultant social interaction between hosts and migrants, the equilibrium is restored by a process of mutual 'adjustment'. The migrants gradually learn to 'adapt' to the values and expectations of the host culture, and for their part the hosts slowly 'accept' the migrants as permanent members of the society. As migrants – or their descendants – are socialised into the dominant values, and as misunderstandings are increasingly resolved, so the newcomers are incorporated into the over-arching consensus.

(e) The process of adjustment may be broken into a discernible sequence of 'stages' in which the spatial and social distance between hosts and newcomers is progressively shortened. Park, for example, described a 'race relations cycle', moving from the initial stage of 'contact' to 'competition' (over jobs, houses, political power), then 'accommodation' (peaceful co-existence) and finally 'assimilation'.

(f) The journey to full 'assimilation' does not necessarily proceed at a regular pace in every sphere of social life, and it may drag over several generations. Yinger (1981) described assimilation as a process of 'boundary reduction' between groups, and he suggests that it involves the following sub-processes: amalgamation (a biological matter, whereby differences in physical appearances are blurred through inter-marriage); identification (a psychological matter, in which feelings of allegiance and commitment to the host society are formed); acculturation (the process of change towards greater cultural similarity); and integration (a structural matter, whereby formerly separate sub-groups become inter-locked in a set of shared interactions).

Having outlined these broad defining features of the model, it is instructive to examine critically a particular example of a study informed by its assumptions.

Dark Strangers

Dark Strangers (Patterson, 1965) is the title of one of the first and most carefully researched studies of West Indians, those living in the

Brixton area of London in the 1950s. It provides a fascinating counter-part to the quite different account of racial conflict in Brixton provided by the Scarman Report on the Brixton Disorders of April, 1981.

Despite the modest disclaimer that her book offers only a rather 'impressionistic' picture, Patterson's assiduous fieldwork resulted in a wealth of observations, and she made a sustained effort to develop a more rigorous sociological understanding of migration and its attendant problems and processes. Patterson's argument is especially striking in its early abandonment of 'colour' as a central issue. Her research experience in South Africa and in the West Indies suggested that the notion of a 'colour bar' was a natural point of entry into the problems. Nevertheless, she argued that the immigrant-host frame-work offered a more serviceable and relevant orientation to the field:

> ... what we have in Britain at the present stage is not, or not yet, basically a colour or a race situation, however much it may appear so to many colour-conscious migrants – it is an immigrant situation. Although colour is a significant 'complicating factor', the essential point about West Indian migrants is precisely the fact that they are migrants, and their problems are little different from those facing any other group of migrants ... The new West Indian migrants to Britain are, in fact, passing through the same kinds of dynamic processes, for example, as the East European Jews and the Irish in London in the last century, the Italians in Canada, the Puerto Ricans in New York, or even the southern rural Negroes in the urban north of the United States.

Patterson identified a cultural gap between the newcomers and hosts, in spite of superficial similarities of language and religion. In Brixton, the white population largely upheld 'respectable' norms which stress privacy, 'keeping themselves to themselves', cleanliness and tidiness, quietness and family propriety. But, she pointed out, 'No immigrant group has in the mass so signally failed to conform to these expectations and patterns as have the West Indians'. The newcomers tended to be more noisy and gregarious, less fastidious about house-keeping standards, and they had a higher proportion of common-law marriages. These departures from 'normal' expectations inevitably caused tensions between the two communities. Nevertheless, West Indians were described as having 'assimilationist' aspirations, and Patterson believed eventual assimilation was possible if both new-comers and hosts made appropriate efforts. The West Indians faced the task of 'adaptation', in which they were to undergo re-socialisation and acculturation into British ways. This involved, among other things, learning to queue at bus stops, formal marriage ceremonies, not building up exaggerated expectations, and the avoidance of 'chip-on-the-shoulder' attitudes. As for the hosts, they are presented with the more 'passive' role of 'acceptance' of the newcomers. The media should avoid lurid, sensational headlines on race issues; people needed to learn not to stare at West Indians in the street; everyone should be treated according to individual merits rather than group membership; and hosts must make an effort to learn more about the newcomers' cultural backgrounds. Patterson remained reasonably optimistic about the prospects for assimilation, because she believed there were no insuperable structural blocks which might stand in the way. Although Britain was an insular, conservative society, it was basically stable and peaceful, with social relationships 'harmonious and voluntarily ordered among the great majority of the society's members'. Also, although mild 'antipathy' to foreigners was a cultural norm, there was an absence of rigid, entrenched prejudice. She argued that emphasis on the 'prejudice-discrimination axis' overlooks the relatively favourable attitudes towards coloured people; and where discrimination did occur it was often for ostensibly 'good' reasons (e.g. 'other tenants would object'; 'children of a mixed marriage would suffer social stigma'; 'too many blacks would upset the white labour force', etc.) which made some sense, at least as far as the white respondents saw the situation. Patterson hoped these 'reasons' would eventually disappear, but she did not view them simply as insincere rationalisations for deep-rooted racism.

Patterson's study did not present a picture of a fixed or an inevitable pattern of absorption and change. On the contrary, a picture was presented that is fluid in the extreme. Yet the underlying assumption – the 'hope factor' informing the study – was that through various stages of varying difficulties a process of assimilation was possible and manageable.

Patterson cautioned that 'adaptation' and 'acceptance' need not always match up with each other, and absorption would not necessarily proceed in a smooth and unbroken fashion. Moreover, the process would move at a different pace in different spheres of life. Based on her own field study in Brixton, Patterson reached the considered conclusion that the situation could be summarised as: 'A fair degree of migrant accommodation in work, somewhat less in housing, and the modest beginnings of migrant acclimatisation and local acquiescence in casual and formal social contacts.' Although most West Indians were semi-skilled or unskilled, and although they suffered from unofficial 'quota' systems by employers, most had managed to find work and had started to accommodate themselves to the disciplines and demands of British industrial life. And in housing, they had managed to overcome a long standing housing shortage and a more recent 'colour tax' whereby unscrupulous landlords asked higher rentals for old and dilapidated property. In the sphere of voluntary social relations, less progress had been made, and there was relatively little contact or mutual understanding between black and white groups. Still, Patterson hazarded the guess that the West Indian population would follow in the footsteps of the Irish towards more complete absorption, gradually raising their living standards and fanning out from the central areas of residential concentration. However, she did recognise that the situation was 'dynamic and uncrystallised', and she insisted that a laissez-faire policy was not sufficient; she made a plea for anti-discrimination legislation, and she advocated more positive state policies to ease the absorption of the newcomers.

Beyond the Immigrant-Host Model

Patterson's careful 1950s study is one of a number informed by the immigrant-host framework. Michael Banton was another who could see positive strength in the methods of enquiry it entailed, whilst doubting its underlying assumptions and the predictions to which it gave rise:

> The racial situation in Britain could develop in any of several different ways. Whether events will approximate more closely to an interpretation in terms of immigration and assimilation, or to one which envisages movement towards a pluralistic pattern of racial communities preserving their distinctiveness in respect of marriage and leisure-time associations, will be decided by the reception accorded to the present second generation of immigrant children when they leave school. This is not a long time to wait for an answer, for it has been estimated that by 1978 one in six of the school-leavers in Birmingham will be a young coloured person. When the second generation leaves the schools it will no longer be possible to represent race relations in Britain as a matter of immigration, or to see coloured people as strangers who could be sent back to their own countries. Thus the image of the coloured man will be modified. Will the pattern of social distance be modified? (Banton, 1967.)

Banton's questions are challenges to the *assumptions* in the immigrant-host framework. Indeed, a number of criticisms can be levelled at the model: (1) its inadequate description of 'stages' of adjustment; (2) its relatively unsophisticated advancement of 'assimilation' as a policy goal; (3) its under-estimation of the extent of 'prejudice' and 'discrimination'; and (4) its theoretically underdeveloped sense of 'social structure'.

(1) **Stages of adjustment.** Rather confusingly, Park referred to a race relations 'cycle' (presumably a pattern which repeats itself) and yet he also described the path to assimilation as a 'progressive' and 'irreversible' sequence. This initial uncertainty is a continuing feature of much immigrant-host literature: on the one hand, there is a basic optimism about a smooth, definite trend towards inter-racial harmony; on the other hand, there is a quite sensible appreciation of the possibility of stops and starts, long pauses, and even some regrettable reversals. It would be rather unfair, perhaps, to condemn the approach for this lack of precision – reality is, after all, highly complex – but the basic concepts ('acceptance', 'accommodation', etc.) are not clearly spelled out, and in practice it remains difficult to identify the exact stage of 'adjustment' which has been reached.

(2) **Assimilation.** The in-built assumption that assimilation is the 'natural' or 'desirable' goal has also been subjected to criticism. It seems that the anticipated adjustment is rather one-way, with the migrants being expected to take on the values and norms of the receiving society, and this overlooks the potential of their own cultural contributions. A clue to the possible benefits of 'cultural exchange' or 'cultural enlargement' (rather than one-way assimilation) is provided by the following comments on British society: 'While it has developed most admirable qualities of self-discipline, professionalism, self-containment, considerateness to others and respect for the law, it has failed fully to develop such other qualities as emotional warmth, psychic openness, capacity to uncoil and relax, ability to enjoy human diversity, generosity of spirit and the like.' (Parekh, 1978.) Moreover, the model normally underestimates the desire by migrants and their descendants to maintain their original cultures (see Chapter 4 on 'ethnicity'). If this is the case, then 'cultural pluralism' is more likely than 'cultural assimilation'. And even if the migrant groups do wish to achieve full (cultural and structural) integration, then they may be prevented from doing so by formidable forces such as widespread prejudice and the intractable structural features of British society.

(3) **Prejudice and discrimination.** The attempt to break away from 'colour' (or the black-white framework) and focus instead on migrant

status was useful insofar as it enlarged understanding of relevant factors, but in the final reckoning it was unrealistic to relegate 'race' or 'colour' to minor significance. In the United States, for example, blacks have largely remained submerged in the 'underclass' for some centuries while successive waves of white migrants (Irish, Poles, Scandinavians) have leapfrogged to prosperity. And in Britain, research (Daniel, 1967) has revealed that white migrants (Cypriots, Hungarians) do not face problems of the same magnitude as those encountered by coloured groups. And so Allen (1971) has interpreted the re-definition of Britain's coloured population as 'immigrants' as little more than a rationalisation which seeks to avoid the brutal fact of racial prejudice. Racial prejudice in Britain has a long history, dating from the earlier settlements in the mid-sixteenth century. Since this period, Walvin (1973) argues, 'with the odd exception, white responses have been bounded on one side by open and legally approved cruelty and on the other by indifference and moral insensibility'. Writers working in the immigrant-host tradition certainly recognised the existence of prejudice and discrimination, but their under-estimation of these factors was starkly revealed by painstaking documentation of their massive and widespread presence in the 1960s and 1970s (see Chapter 3).

(4) **Social structure.** Conflict theorists argue that the immigrant-host model suffers from the limitations of a 'consensus' or 'order' view of society. In other words, it assumes a basic harmony of interests and values in the host society; it tends to view immigration as posing a problem of 'adjustment' because of the clash of values and consequent 'mutual misunderstandings'; and it frames the solution very much in terms of re-socialisation and cultural integration. Against this conception, the critics maintain that a conflict view of race (Horton, 1966) offers a more informative and analytically useful understanding of the relevant forces at work. For the conflict theorists, Britain is a sharply divided, class-stratified society in which different interest groups contest a struggle for power. The disadvantaged position of coloured migrants is explained by their historical role as cheap labour, and their continued exploitation is guaranteed by the racism which capitalism generates to serve its own intersts. The root of the problem, then, does not lie in restricted opportunities due to a clash of values, but in an exploitative economic order which can only be resolved by radical structural transformation (see Chapter 5).

But it is important not to discard the many insights and issues posed by the immigrant-host studies: after all, the New Commonwealth arrivals were, indeed, migrants, and Krausz (1971) illustrates the many parallels in the migration patterns and attendant problems of black and white migrants. The model effectively drew attention to the dislocation caused by migration, it bravely addressed the complexities of assimilation, and it demonstrated the dynamic processes of change, rather than settling for a misleadingly static view of black-white conflict. Also, it stood as a reminder that the migrants brought different sets of cultural values, and inevitably this raised important policy issues of how far cultural diversity could be accommodated within one nation state. So the model insisted that there were phenomena to be explained and problems to be solved. If it failed to supply satisfactory answers to all the issues, at least it stimulated further development of the debates.

In the next chapter we will shift focus from the migrants to the hosts and explore the latter's racial prejudices and discriminatory practices.

Chapter Three

Racism

Within the immigrant-host framework the expectation was that, after an initial phase of hostility, familiarity would promote mutual respect, and immigrants would merge – become *integrated* – into British society. A famous definition of 'integration' was provided by a Labour Party Home Secretary: 'not a flattening process of assimilation, but equal opportunity, accompanied by cultural diversity, in an atmosphere of mutual tolerance' (Jenkins, 1967). Nevertheless, in spite of these lofty intentions it became clear that relations between 'hosts' and 'immigrants' were marked by continuing hostility and intolerance. And that is why the concept of 'prejudice' became central to a great deal of research and theory in race relations. This tradition of 'prejudice' studies deserves special attention.

Prejudice

In the strict dictionary sense, it is possible to be prejudiced in favour of a group, but in social science the term is normally reserved for derogatory attitudes, as in the following frequently cited definition:

> An avertive or hostile attitude towards a person who belongs to a group, simply because he belongs to that group, and is therefore presumed to have the objectionable characteristics ascribed to the group. (Allport, 1954.)

This definition furnishes a basis for identifying some of the key features of prejudice:

(1) Prejudice consists of negative 'attitudes' or 'beliefs' which are directed at some 'out-group'. Of course, not every out-group is denounced or pitied, but anything which marks off a group as 'different' makes it a potential target for disapproval.

(2) As the term suggests, an element of pre-judgement is involved. Instead of treating people on their individual merits, they are portrayed in terms of misleading stereotypes which allow little room for fairmindedness or sensible negotiation.

(3) A certain amount of stereotyping is inevitable and even necessary in social relationships, but prejudice is additionally unfair because it involves a strong measure of mis-judgement as well. For instance, the objectionable 'differences' may be imagined or highly exaggerated, and the attractive features of the group may be totally ignored.

(4) Some people subscribe to racial prejudices because they have been misinformed or have fallen prey to common misconceptions in their culture. Nevertheless, the race debate is not a neutral, dispassionate affair which is easily resolved by patient regard for the available evidence. Prejudices involve emotions and feelings as well as simple information; indeed, some psychologists suggest that prejudiced people have underlying personality needs which lead them to denounce others.

Clearly, there are a large number of candidates for the unenviable role of 'victim': gypsies, foreigners, Jews, sexual minorities, left-wingers, right-wingers, dwarves, even sociologists. But the field of race relations provides particularly rich examples of the potent nature of prejudice. Here are some common prejudiced stereotypes: Asians are seen as 'shifty' and 'cunning', and stand condemned for alleged avarice and low standards of physical hygiene. Their 'alien' presence is signalled by their apparently incomprehensible languages, 'heathen' religions, impenetrable cultures, and their 'enslavement' of women. For West Indians, the stereotypes often draw a link to criminality with special emphasis on the phenomenon of 'mugging', or dwell on noisy music, drug taking and wild parties. Such stereotypes have a long history, and even as far back as the 18th century the British had formed discrediting or patronising views of the African: 'The Negro was held to be peculiarly sexual, musical, stupid, indolent, untrustworthy and violent.' (Walvin, 1973.)
Sometimes the selected features which are seized on are patently false (differences in intelligence, for instance), but the more subtle and sinister stereotype is that which starts from something real, but distorts it out of all recognition. So the Asian cultural emphasis on the extended family and on village ties undergoes a curious transformation: it is alleged that they actually prefer to live in overcrowded conditions!

Such a mischievous claim not only stigmatises the group as 'primitive' in their standards, but it conveniently overlooks the structural conditions which force many Asian families in Britain to live – reluctantly – in less than ideal conditions.

Another strange feature of racial prejudice is that the characteristics which are condemned in others are not always obviously discrediting. The alleged sexual prowess or musical talents of West Indians, for example, might be expected to elicit grudging admiration in some quarters. And the 'clannish' tendencies and mutual aid patterns found among Asian groups are not very distant from the qualities celebrated in 'traditional' working-class culture in Britain. Yet these qualities, when supposedly discovered in other 'races', are framed in a slanted way: the sexually prodigious blacks contribute to high rape and illegit- imacy rates; their otherwise admirable spontaneity tends to lead to all- night parties which disturb their white neighbours; the clannish Asians are supposedly using their social networks to conspire against us. Moreover, the irrational element in racial prejudice is readily demon- strated by the inconsistency of popular attitudes. Thus, West Indians are criticised for (allegedly) being lazy and workshy, while Asians are blamed for the opposite reason that they are supposedly too hard- working ('they steal our jobs and grab all the overtime they can get'). Whatever they do – or are believed to do – they cannot win.

Studying Prejudice

There were a number of studies in the 1960s which tried to measure the extent of prejudice against coloured immigrants. Character- istically, the study of prejudice entails asking a sample of the population whether they agree or disagree with a list of positive and negative statements about groups of people. Then the responses are analysed by scoring the number which are prejudiced or unprejudiced and then distributing the population into groups with low or high scores.

One of the most ambitious surveys of this type was included in a massive study by the Institute of Race Relations in the late 1960s (Rose, 1969). After submitting a questionnaire to two thousand five hundred whites in five towns in England, the researchers concluded that thirty-five per cent of the sample displayed 'no hostility', a further fifty-five per cent shared 'doubts and uncertainties', while the remaining ten per cent were described as 'intensely prejudiced'. The latter group were more likely to be found among the lower middle-class and skilled working class, among Conservatives, the poorly educated, those with little personal contact with migrants, and among those with 'authoritarian' personalities. Overall, however, the findings did not present too bleak a picture, since they seemed to indicate that pronounced racial prejudice was not widespread. Indeed, it was suggested that 'what is needed (in short) is not an effort to make people unprejudiced, but rather to remind them that they are unprejudiced'. But more recently, in a 1984 report on British social attitudes, the apparently larger figure of thirty-five per cent of the sample identified themselves as 'racially prejudiced' (Jowell & Airey, 1984).

Plainly, there are recurrent methodological problems associated with this kind of survey, and so the results always need to be treated with caution. Apart from the obvious matter of the representativeness of the sample, sensitive and probing questions are required, otherwise the answers will be uninformative or positively misleading. Bald figures or head-counts – ten per cent belong to this group, twenty per cent to that group, etc. – are usually less revealing than a more detailed analysis of the underlying processes. If, for example, we investigate the 'doubts and uncertainties' group, some interesting tensions are disclosed. On the basis of her fieldwork in London in the 1950s, Ruth Glass (1960) aptly described this group as holding attitudes of 'benevolent prejudice'. Far from being severely hostile or unfailingly sympathetic towards ethnic minorities, they were typically muddled, confused and insecure. Their ambivalent outlook was a curious blend of competing values, of passive tolerance and latent prejudice, and different situations determined which element prevailed at any given time. For Glass, there was an urgent need to develop a 'philosophy of tolerance' to help overcome the 'sluggishness of good will' and prevent the mobilisation of intolerance.

Glass's sensitive exploration of the social climate of prejudice illustrates the value of moving beyond simple quantitative methods and mere head-counting. This is not, of course, to deny the role of attitude surveys in providing useful data on how people actually feel, and in acting as some sort of empirical check on otherwise unsupported claims about the extent of prejudice. But there is a danger that the 'snapshot' approach of these surveys freezes people and situations in too rigid a fashion. The temptation is to regard people as rather fixed in their attitudes ('some people are like this', 'some people are like that') and thereby overlook the extent to which their attitudes (and personalities) may be shaped by their cultural heritage and social circumstances. If these circumstances change, so we might expect some degree of movement in the profile of opinions and beliefs in the population.

Another criticism of these surveys is that the attitudes expressed do not always provide a reliable indication of how people are likely to behave in real-life situations. But the most important criticism of the 'prejudice' approach is the way in which it reduces the issues to the level of 'individuals'.

Sociologists accept that some individuals are more inclined than others towards prejudice, but they challenge the notion that racial hostility is basically a matter of the idiosyncratic attitudes and behaviour of a small number of disturbed personalities. In a country like Britain, for example, racial prejudice is far from being the exclusive property of a few scattered bigots. Just by growing up in this society, by incorporating its culture and history, and by being exposed to the mass media, many 'normal' people will become familiar with negative racial stereotypes. Prejudice, then, is enshrined within popular cultural traditions and dominant social institutions; it is not a matter of the free-floating attitudes of a few individuals. Furthermore, the causes of prejudice are not limited to the search for a 'prejudice-prone personality' or a few key 'psychological' factors. A major task of sociology is to demonstrate how the level and intensity of racial prejudice in a society responds to shifting social forces and power struggles. For example, where there is a social situation of economic or political conflict, the flames of prejudice are likely to be fanned. So we can see that sociologists shift the focus away from abstract 'attitudes' or 'personality dynamics' towards a wider social canvas. Prejudice is located within a social and historical context, and it is there that the major causes are identified. If racial 'prejudice' is the individualistic notion studied by psychologists, sociologists focus on *racism*. Three distinct uses of this term can be identified.

Racism

1. Racism as Ideology – Cultural Racism

Most commonly, 'racism' refers to a whole cluster of cultural ideas, beliefs and arguments which transmit mistaken notions about the attributes and capabilities of 'racial' groups. The term indicates a generally available cultural complex which falsely claims that certain 'races' (often fanciful) are condemned to a permanent position of moral, cultural and intellectual inferiority. The racist beliefs may be consciously incorporated within some pseudo-scientific doctrine, and indeed Banton (1977) has proposed that the term strictly applies only to those 'biological' explanations of racial inferiority – or theories of racial typology – which flourished in the nineteenth century. However, most sociologists prefer to adopt a broader and looser formulation of racism.

Rex (1970), for example, states that racism is present whenever any 'deterministic belief system' regards group characteristics as narrowly 'fixed' and therefore leading inevitably to rather rigid and exclusive barriers between one group and another. The belief system may well take the form of an explicitly 'scientific' theory (based on biology or psychometrics), but other grounds are possible. Thus, apartheid in South Africa is currently defended on the dubious grounds of alleged 'cultural' and 'historical' differences, without any obvious reference to biological arguments. Alternatively, corrupted theological doctrines may be employed to justify racial disadvantage (e.g. the argument that God purposely created different tribes, or that black suffering is the result of God's curse on the descendants of Ham). In addition to these systematic doctrines, however, racism may appear also at the less ordered and more inconsistent level of 'folk wisdom' or 'common-sense'. But even at this level the presence of racism can be related to structural and historical factors (e.g. history of British Empire).

2. Racism as Practice – Racialism

The term 'racism' is also used to refer to behaviour, policies or types of treatment which are informed by racial antipathies. This includes individual acts (a white employer refusing a job to a black applicant simply because he is black) and institutional policies (local authority refusing to make reasonable housing provisions for ethnic minorities). Prejudice does not just lurk inside the minds of people: it also finds expression in the ways they treat one another. Unfortunately, the use of the term 'racism' in this sense leads to complications since 'racism' then refers not only to ideas and beliefs rooted in culture, but also to 'behaviour' influenced by these beliefs.

It seems far less confusing to reserve the term 'racism' for the cultural attitude and observe the usual convention of adopting the term 'racial discrimination' or 'racialism' to describe the differential treatment of racial groups. We should note, however, that some schools of thought avoid such a distinction. So for Stuart Hall, writing in a neo-Marxist vein, racism is 'a set of economic, political and ideological practices' (Hall, 1980).

However, there is no direct link between racism (the attitude) and racialism (the behaviour). It is quite possible, for example, to imagine a white Afrikaaner reluctantly complying with apartheid because of possible sanctions against him (racialism without racism). However, racism and racialism are likely to feed each other in circular fashion. People who harbour prejudices are likely to find that it influences the way they act towards minority groups, no matter how much they try to conceal their feelings. And the behaviour also influences attitudes: if people are in the habit of treating minorities badly, then they will find that their negative attitudes are reinforced. If, for example, a minority racial group is habitually refused decent jobs, housing or education, then its resultant low standards of living will appear to justify the initial prejudice ('they must deserve it').

3. Racism as Social Structure – Institutional Racism

This version depicts racism as an enduring structural feature of a society, recognisable by social patterns of disadvantage and inequality which run along racial lines. Thus, Mason (1982) defines institutional racism as: 'any situation in which groups, socially defined as races, are systematically disadvantaged in respect of social rewards, capacities or opportunities'.

So alongside cultural racism (beliefs and attitudes) and racialism (differential treatment) we must place institutional racism, which draws attention to the ways in which racism penetrates the dominant organisations and power structure of society, resulting in distinctive patterns of social disadvantage. Racist assumptions are enshrined as the working basis for major institutions and official bodies; racialism becomes entrenched in routine procedures and rules.

Carmichael and Hamilton (1969) make a dramatic distinction between 'individual racism' and 'institutional racism':

> When white terrorists bomb a black church and kill five black children, that is an act of individual racism, widely deplored by most segments of the society. But when in that same city – Birmingham, Alabama – five hundred black babies die each year because of the lack of proper food, shelter and medical facilities, and thousands more are destroyed and maimed physically, emotionally and intel- lectually because of conditions of poverty and discrim- ination in the black community, that is a function of institu- tional racism. When a black family moves into a home in a white neighbourhood and is stoned, burned or routed out, they are victims of an overt act of individual racism which many people will condemn – at least in words. But it is institutional racism that keeps black people in dilapidated slum tenements, subject to the daily prey of exploitative slumlords, merchants, loan sharks and discriminatory real estate agents.

But certain difficulties arise if we stray from the purely descriptive level of using the term 'institutional racism' to indicate objective patterns of social disadvantage. For example, do the social institutions deliberately discriminate along racial lines ('conspiracy version')? Is institutional racism simply the accidental by-product of non-racist decisions ('unintended consequences version')? Mason draws attention to these and other rival versions and shows how these differing interpretations make it difficult to 'prove' the existence of institutional racism satisfactorily. Because of the ambiguities surrounding the term, there is a danger of it being employed as a political slogan rather than as an analytical tool.

The task now remains to decide whether modern Britain can be described as a 'racist' society.

Measuring Racism

Walvin (1984) notes that racial animosity and discrimination are not new in Britain. On the contrary, they are all too visible in the troubled history of black people in this country since the sixteenth century. Nevertheless, it is not an easy task to chart the ebb and flow of the tide of racism, nor to assess the depth and range of the problem at any given time. Invariably we are left with imprecise measures and rough estimates, and even then the 'factual' results are selectively interpreted according to the values and theoretical positions of those who enter the debate. Take, for example, the following two judgements:

> In talking about racist resentment, I did not at all wish to suggest that Britain is a racist society, nor that every Briton is a racist. Such a suggestion would be utterly false and grossly unfair. When all is said and done, Britain is one of the most decent and civilised societies in the world, and is characterised by a considerable sense of fairness and humanity (Parekh, 1978).

> Our record of tolerance is clearly not compatible with our image of ourselves as a liberal and tolerant nation... we must divest ourselves of the comforting myth of our national tolerance and painfully recognise that Britain is an endemically racist society (Husband, 1975).

These conclusions stem from ultimately contrasting images of society. Clearly, the 'radical' who adopts a conflict model is far more likely to regard entrenched racism as the inevitable outcome of a basically exploitative society; those who adopt 'liberal' or 'pluralist' models are attracted towards a more 'balanced' picture of the good and bad features of British race relations; and for extreme 'right-wingers' the problem is not racism at all but the presence of 'alien' people on British soil. These contrasting interpretations have to be remembered when examining the following empirical evidence.

(a) Cultural Racism

The association of dark skin with social inferiority is deep-rooted in our cultural heritage. Some writers relate this association to basic structures of thought and language which, for example, are expressed in the universal contrast between night and day, dirt and cleanliness, good and evil. This means that blackness stands as a symbolic representation of the things we fear or hold in contempt. Fryer (1984) illustrates these connections:

> The very words 'black' and 'white' were heavily charged with meaning long before the English met people whose skins were black. Blackness, in England, traditionally stood for death, mourning, baseness, evil, sin and danger. It was the colour of bad magic, melancholy, and the nethermost pit of hell. People spoke of black arts, blackmail, and the Black Death . . . White, on the other hand, was the colour of purity, virginity, innocence, good magic, flags of truce, harmless lies, and perfect human beauty.

Nevertheless, the expansion in geographical 'discoveries' and inter-racial contact from the sixteenth century on prompted the creation of further images and additional myths. For example, Walvin (1978) documents the influential role of returned travellers in popularising fanciful stereotypes and circulating lurid tales about foreign races. Patronising attitudes towards these 'primitive', 'innocent' and 'ignorant' people rested alongside more alarmist descriptions of their 'savage', 'heathen', and 'promiscuous' habits. And later, during the rapid expansion of the British Empire in the late nineteenth century, writers like Kipling fired the public imagination with vivid portraits of 'new-caught sullen peoples, half-devil and half-child', who apparently lagged well behind the British 'race' in civilised behaviour and nobility of mind. The remarkable accomplishments of the colonial powers certainly offered plausible support for spurious claims of white superiority. And the experience of colonial subjugation and enslave-ment imposed a lasting stigma on people with dark skins. History therefore provides a potent range of racial imagery, and this cultural legacy has been passed on to succeeding generations in varying forms (creative literature, school textbooks, pseudo-scientific theories, general folk-lore).

But it is misleading to regard cultural racism as merely some curiously influential survival from the colonial past. Culture is not normally handed down in an untampered form, but is constantly being re-created and transformed. Cultural racism, then, consists of a shifting network of interlocking ideas, images and assumptions, and each generation contributes to the re-shaping of this cultural complex. In modern Britain, for example, the imperial myths have hardly been swallowed wholesale; there are various counter-currents (intellectual and religious traditions, political ideologies, even the decent sentiments of the 'benevolently prejudiced') which represent a challenge to the dominance of racist assumptions. But we also have to recognise new sources and manifestations of cultural prejudices. Thus, a recent report by the Policy Studies Institute (1983) discovered that racial prejudice and racial talk are pervasive in the Metropolitan Police Force. The researchers found that a rhetoric of racial abuse ('nigger', 'coon', 'wog') was not only tolerated but actually cultivated in the occupational cultures of police, a group holding a powerful and publicly sensitive position. Likewise, the mass media have been identified as a particularly insidious source of racist sentiments (Hartmann and Husband, 1974). They have been accused of treating blacks in Britain as alien 'outsiders' and therefore as a 'problem' rather than an asset. Instead of vigorously condemning white racism, they have exaggerated immigration figures; instead of investigating the underprivileged conditions of blacks in this country, they have spot-lighted black crime rates. Admittedly, the media do not present a uniform picture, and no doubt counter-examples could be found. But the media are important shapers of public opinion, so any biases in their presentation are a serious cause for concern. Another source for cultural racism lies in the materials used by schools in socialising the young to a view of history and other cultures. A constant strand of complaint from parents of ethnic minority children relates to how the school curriculum ignores their presence and even reinforces racism. 'Little Black Sambo' remains alive and well in dozens of storybooks; the glories of imperial conquest are daily celebrated in classrooms; the superiority of the Christian over other religions is expressed in insensitive ways. By sketching how a school system can perpetuate, or at least not challenge, cultural stereotypes of a racist nature, we start to show how cultural racism becomes institutionalized.

(b) Racialism

Simply asking hypothetical questions in an opinion survey does not in itself establish how people actually behave towards one another.

Even the previously-mentioned report on the Metropolitan Police did not claim that they acted in a consistently discriminatory manner towards minority groups. So independent evidence has to be unearthed in order to assess the extent of racial discrimination in this country. Firm evidence for the widespread nature of racialism is provided by a painstaking series of studies conducted by Political and Economic Planning (PEP), a research organisation which later merged in the Policy Studies Institute (PSI). In an early PEP study (Daniel, 1968), a wide battery of research methods was employed. Apart from questionnaires and interviews with random samples of 'whites' and 'coloureds', the researchers investigated a selected group of 500 'potential discriminators' (e.g. recruitment personnel, building society managers, landlords). In addition, they developed the useful ruse of 'situation tests', where they sent professional actors (representing a white Englishman, a Hungarian or Cypriot migrant, and a coloured migrant) after the same job or flat. The disturbing conclusion was that racial discrimination ranged 'from the substantial to the massive' in many spheres: employment, housing, and services such as insurance, banking, shops and building societies. Coloured migrants were clearly less successful in applications for jobs, bank loans, mortgages and other valued resources. Also, far from being over-sensitive, they actually underestimated the amount of racial discrimination they suffered. And this discrimination could not be explained away by 'rational' criteria such as inferior qualifications (the better-educated were likely to experience an even greater degree of job discrimination!). A similar PEP study in the mid-1970s (Smith, 1977) concluded that racial discrimination had diminished to some extent. Nevertheless, there was still marked discrimination in the job market (especially for non-manual and unskilled workers), in privately-rented accommodation, and in the council house sector (where migrants were allocated inferior accommodation).

Both of these PEP reports strengthened the case for firmer anti-discrimination legislation. The second report indicated that earlier legislation (e.g. the 1965 Race Relations Act) had made some impact, but it also provided documented proof that discrimination still persisted. In recognition of this stubborn persistence, the 1976 Race Relations Act broadened the scope of legislation to restrict practices which, irrespective of intention, had the effect of discriminating against ethnic minorities (e.g. laying down rigorous but unnecessary language qualifications for manual jobs). Nevertheless, the history of government measures to outlaw discrimination and promote racial harmony is hardly an unqualified success. Dummett and Dummett (1982) argue that successive British governments must accept the major blame for continued racialism in this country. Instead of endorsing the notion of a truly multi-cultural, multi-racial society, governments have increasingly offered concessions to mounting racist demands. Instead of launching a concerted campaign against racism and against racially motivated attacks on blacks, they have passed a series of immigration laws which enshrine racist assumptions: blacks are seen as a 'problem' and their numbers must be limited; white 'patrials' are perfectly acceptable, but the 'alien' invasion threatens to 'swamp' the country. Quite apart from the distress caused to separated relatives, the harsh enforcement of immigration laws convinces the 'hesitant, ambivalent and confused' whites that they were right to feel apprehensive, and it encourages racists to make fresh demands. Governments have certainly maintained a 'respectable' face by passing relatively toothless and ill-designed anti-discrimination legislation, but many of their own practices simply reinforce racialism. Their positive measures have not radically altered the patterns of social disadvantage which the black population continue to suffer.

(c) Institutional Racism

The main preoccupation in the PEP/PSI studies gradually shifted from concern with 'prejudice' and 'discrimination' towards the documentation of the social patterns of disadvantage among Britain's black population. This shift was signalled in Smith's 1974 report which noted that disadvantage stems from various sources, not from discrimination alone. For example, the language problems of migrants might hamper their economic progress; and once migrants are recruited as a replacement population in the less prestigious jobs, the 'normal' structural features of British society (class differentials in power and opportunities) may result in the perpetuation of disadvantage. Obviously, then, it was important not to confuse discrimination and disadvantage, and the plotting of 'life chances' assumed a new priority. The 1974 report duly confirmed the underprivileged status of black migrants and their British-born descendants. Although there were interesting differences between the various 'ethnic' groups, the broad job picture was clear. Black males were over-represented in manual jobs, especially in the semi-skilled and unskilled sectors; they earned less than their white counterparts, and they were more likely to work shifts. In the housing sphere, blacks tended to be concentrated in less desirable areas of cities. Tenure patterns did not immediately suggest disadvantage – 'Asians', for example, were more likely than whites to be owner-occupiers – but the quality of housing was generally poorer, both in the private and the public sector. Overall, the gap between blacks and whites was clearly marked in most spheres of life.

A Home Office review (Field, 1981) of authoritative research findings criticised the PEP report for over-sampling inner-city areas, and hence exaggerating the gap between whites and blacks. Taking the period 1961–81, they recorded absolute improvements in the housing and job conditions of the minorities, and offered the following qualified conclusion: 'The trends described certainly do not support the notion of ethnic minorities as constituting a social group barred from all avenues of social progress, but nor do they show gains on all fronts'. But the latest PSI study, based on research in 1982 (Brown, 1984) did avoid over-sampling inner-city areas, and it also included a sample of women for the first time, so its conclusions merit attention. Like the Home Office study, they acknowledged 'considerable improvements' in housing conditions: the high level of owner-occupation has remained steady among Asian groups, while owner-occupation and council tenancy have risen for West Indian groups; there has been a marked decline in household size and overcrowding; there is less sharing of amenities with other households. Against this, there is little sign of any dispersal of the black population (the modest dispersal that has taken place is mainly into adjoining areas previously identifiable as clusters of 'immigrant settlement'). And they conclude that:

> the quality of the housing of black people is much worse than the quality of housing in general in this country. Blacks are more often at higher floor levels, and those with houses are less likely to have detached or semi-detached property; black families have smaller property on average, and, with larger household size, their density of occupation is much higher; black households more often share rooms or amenities with other households; the properties black families own or rent are older; and they are less likely to have a garden.

As for jobs, the only optimistic sign was that the status gap in the jobs secured by young blacks and whites was not so great as in the past. However, in the grim climate of economic recession, the unemployment rates of blacks was up to twice as high as that of whites (in 1974 it had been the same). Elsewhere, little had changed:

> The survey gives us a depressing picture of the economic lives of people of Asian and West Indian origin in Britain today. They are more likely than white people to be unemployed, and those who are in work tend to have jobs with lower pay and lower status than those of white

workers . . . there has been little convergence of the types of
job done by the majority and minority ethnic groups . . .

Overall, then, the 1982 PSI research found little change in the
structural situation of black citizens: the disadvantaged position of the
original migrant workers persisted in the second and subsequent
generations.

In this chapter we have defined some key concepts, and we have
looked at some empirical evidence concerning the problems of 'racism'
in Britain. In order to deepen our understanding of the nature and
meaning of these problems, we must now turn to the more theoretically
informed debates in the following chapters.

Chapter Four

Ethnicity

As we noted in the previous chapter, the immigrant-host model hinged on the belief that migrants from the Caribbean and the Asian sub-continent would eventually become 'acculturated', gradually shedding their distinctive identities and cultural norms, and slowly becoming socialised into the dominant values and folk-ways of the host society. The model, admittedly, conceded that only a modest degree of cultural assimilation was likely for 'primary' settlers, and it recognised that continued 'colour' discrimination might impede the process as far as the second generation was concerned, but nevertheless the envisaged trend was firmly in the direction of a cultural 'melting pot'. However, this framework of assumptions was disturbed in the 1960s and 1970s by the dawning realisation that migrant cultures were not simply short-lived phenomena destined to fade away rapidly under the dual impact of disruptive migration and the seductive attractions of the host culture. On the contrary, migrants and their descendants appeared to be stubbornly retaining many elements of their 'original' cultures, modifying them to only a limited extent, and sometimes emphasising them even more fervently with the passage of time. It became increasingly obvious, therefore, that cultural allegiances – 'ethnicity' – merited special attention.

This rediscovery of the importance of the 'ethnic factor' was not confined to Britain. Several commentators suggested that a process of 'massive retribalisation' was taking place in most Western societies, expressing itself in a renewed awareness of linguistic, religious, cultural and national identities. In the United States, for example, some writers identified a process of 'dissimilation', in which native-born Americans were re-asserting the ethnic traditions of their ancestors. Other cited examples included the persisting 'language divide' in countries like

Canada, Belgium and Wales; mounting religious conflict in Ulster and Holland; and the increased popularity of regional independence movements in nation states like Britain and Spain. These types of issues, it was argued, could not be explained fully by conventional 'political' or 'economic' analysis, since they involved an underlying 'ethnic' or 'cultural' dimension which gave them their special character.

Sociology in the 1950s and 1960s was taken somewhat unawares by these developments, and Burgess (1978) attributes this to the misleading influence of two strands of thought which he calls the 'liberal expectancy' and the 'radical expectancy'. The liberal expectancy had broadly assumed that the processes of modernisation and industrialisation would lead to the early dissolution of 'primitive' ethnic affiliations, as people adopted a more 'rational' and 'individualistic' approach to life. The radical expectancy shared the view that ethnic groups would become superfluous and irrelevant, but it assumed that people would abandon the 'false consciousness' of ethnic groups for the supposedly more 'realistic' arena of class struggle. In this radical scenario, ethnic groups would decline as members aligned themselves with their appropriate social class interests. However, the liberal and radical expectancies were apparently challenged by the train of events implied by 'massive retribalisation', and this prompted fresh academic interest in the whole question of ethnicity.

The Ethnic Dimension

An 'ethnic group' has been defined by Schermerhorn (1970) as 'a collectivity within a larger society, having real or putative ancestry, memories of a shared historical past, and a cultural focus on one or more symbolic elements defined as the epitome of their people-hood'. In a similar vein, Yinger (1981) suggests that the term refers to 'a segment of a larger society whose members are thought, by themselves and/or by others, to share a common origin and to share important segments of a common culture, and who, in addition, participate in shared activities in which the common origin and culture are significant ingredients'. From these definitions we can extract some key features of ethnic groups: shared culture, regular social interaction, and a sense of 'belonging' accompanied by an almost cult-like mystique which secures the bonds of unity between the members. The key term in ethnic studies is 'culture', which Khan (1982) defines as: 'the system of shared meanings developed in a social and economic context which has a particular historical and political background'. Culture is the distinctive 'design for living' that a group possesses, the sum total of its rules and guides for shaping behaviour and patterning its way of life. These cultural bonds can be so strong that when members move from one country to another – as in the case of New Commonwealth migrants to Britain – they frequently make determined efforts to sustain their ethnic identity by pursuing traditional religious and cultural customs, maintaining dietary habits, and keeping alive the languages and dialects of their homelands. It can be anticipated, also, that certain types of social experience and group formation are particularly conducive to the emergence of cleary-defined ethnic groups, and the most familiar examples of ethnic groups are usually based on nations, territorial units, religious codes, common language, and tribal or clan membership. Some writers have further suggested that 'race' is another likely source of 'ethnicity', so that we might expect the boundaries between races to coincide with the boundaries between ethnic groups. However, the connection is not quite that simple, and it needs to be spelled out in greater detail.

Various attempts have been made to establish the relevance of cultural factors in race relations situations. In the United States, especially, there has been a rather long-standing reluctance to acknowledge the cultural distinctiveness of the black population. Following the lead of respected researchers like Frazier and Myrdal, the American black was portrayed first and foremost as an American, thoroughly steeped in American culture. Anxious to combat racist notions, researchers tended to emphasise the cultural similarities of black and whites; alleged features of 'black culture' were explained away as stemming from lower-class culture in general, or from the general cultural milieu of the southern USA, and so it was denied that there was a distinctive 'black culture' at all. Blauner (1972), however, took issue with this dominant line of argument. Blauner insists that the historical experience of slavery, the forced entry into American society, remains a formidable shaping influence in black consciousness. He further argues that there is a recognisable black culture, forged from diverse sources: slavery, the African heritage, and the experience of racism and poverty. Themes like 'soul' and 'survival' are especially prominent, and cannot be regarded as a normal part of the general lower class culture. Moreover, Blauner points out that culture is not something fixed and static: it is constantly being created and re-created, and so black culture was able to incorporate notions like 'Black is Beautiful' and 'Black Power' in the 1960s. Finally, Blauner contends that the denial of a black culture is itself racist, or 'neo-racist', since it refuses to recognise the independent integrity of the black experience.

If it could be argued that blacks in the United States – after centuries of residence in that country – retained a distinctive culture, how much more pertinent the whole question of ethnicity seemed in a country like Britain, with its more recent upsurge in immigration from the New Commonwealth. Consequently, the new emphasis on ethnicity was eagerly borrowed by British race academics.

However, the connection between race and ethnicity is by no means straightforward. In our first chapter we showed the untenable nature of the argument that innate biological characteristics somehow 'determine' the cultural content of the racial group concerned. So, depending on circumstances, people of different 'races' may combine to create a common 'culture'; conversely, people of a given 'race' may create quite different 'cultures'. This means that there is no exact match between 'race' and 'ethnic' group; and so, strictly speaking, the terms should not be used interchangeably. Indeed, Lyon (1972) has attempted to distinguish race and ethnic group analytically. Firstly, an ethnic group is defined culturally, whereas a racial group is physically defined. Secondly, he maintains that an ethnic group voluntarily erects barriers between itself and other groups, whereas a racial group tends to be forcibly excluded and prevented from freely interacting with other groups. Thirdly, Lyon argues that ethnic groups enjoy a sense of solidarity and demonstrate a capacity for mobilisation of their collective interests, whereas racial groups tend to be little more than residual categories which have dim prospects for collective efforts. Lyon's conceptualisation certainly represents a brave attempt to sort out important terms and to avoid confusion, but ultimately it fails to establish a clear distinction. For instance, there is no convincing reason why a racial group cannot be 'self-defined', developing a positive sense of purpose and mutuality, and displaying considerable organisational talents (white racists and Black Power advocates are hardly likely to regard race as a mere residual category!). The experience of racism itself may help forge a unifying cultural identity, as we have already seen in the case of blacks in the United States. Moreover, members of a racial group tend to grow up together, to share common territory and social experiences, and so to that extent we might expect a common culture to emerge. So, in the end, the rigid separation of 'race' and 'ethnic group' cannot be sustained, and that is why the study of ethnicity is potentially so valuable for a deeper understanding of race relations. At its simplest, the underlying argument of this chapter is that race relations in Britain cannot be understood properly without taking due account of the ethnic affiliations of the groups concerned.

Studying Ethnicity

The reorientation in academic studies towards a greater emphasis on ethnicity was a welcome addition to the race relations literature. From the 1960s onwards there was a concerted effort to map out the field of 'ethnic studies', and this resulted in the launching of extremely valuable ethnographic studies of the communities concerned. Researchers carefully documented the distinguishing cultural features of selected groups of New Commonwealth migrants, charting the ways in which these groups differed in such things as language, religion, core values and social attitudes, kinship patterns, diet and routine life styles. Meanwhile, there was an increasing appreciation of the sheer complexity of cultural adaptation as migrants moved from one culture to another. This process could not be described as a simple matter of complete 'assimilation', but neither was it a matter of successfully preserving the 'original' culture intact. The process of adaptation was additionally complicated by the position of the second generation, who were frequently described as caught 'between two cultures' (Watson, 1977). In order to understand the transitions and upheavals entailed, Lea and Young (1984) suggest we must consider:

(1) The culture of the country (e.g. India, Jamaica) from which migration takes place.

(2) The particular sub-culture of those who migrate (e.g. Sikh Punjabis, Hindu Punjabis).

(3) The sub-cultures (e.g. second generation youth cultures) which spring up as part of the shifting process of adaptation to the country of immigration.

Lea and Young also take pains to warn against the dangers of assuming that the migrant culture is homogeneous (e.g. there will be generational, sexual and social class variations on cultural themes). Moreover, the view that ethnicity is somehow a desperate hanging-on to some archaic or 'primitive' or inappropriate form of 'life ways' is one that must be treated critically. Indeed, as we shall see, an important strength of some studies is how they describe and explain the *new* forms of communal life which emerge in multicultural Britain.

By considering some recent ethnographic studies we can explore these aspects further.

Sketches from Contemporary Ethnographic Studies

(1) Pakistanis

Pakistani communities, both in Britain and in Pakistan itself, have been subjected to close study by *Khan* (1977) and by *Dahya* (1973). By reaching beyond the normal confines of ethnographic research to include both 'home' and 'host' societies, this allows them to trace interesting continuities and discontinuities entailed in the process of migration. But the subtle process of change and adaptation is not merely a mechanical response to new circumstances or external constraints. Rather, the subjective attitudes, intentions and aspirations of the migrants themselves help shape the outcome in important ways. The favoured lifestyles and cultural affiliations of the ethnic groups concerned influence their experiences in Britain.

Most Pakistani migrants to Britain are drawn from the rural areas of the Punjab, Campbellpur and Mirpur. Khan describes the typical village life and cultural features of the Mirpuris, who inhabit the Kashmir region yet speak a Punjabi dialect. The typical household consists of three generations, with the eldest male having the greatest authority. The extended family has great importance, and frequently marriage takes place between cousins. Like most South Asian groups, arranged marriages are the norm. The Mirpuris belong to the Sunni sect of Islam, and women are expected to observe the regulations of purdah (involving wearing the veil, shunning the company of male strangers, etc.). Nevertheless, the general respect shown to traditional customs allows women to participate in the normal round of gregarious outdoor village life. Overall, there is a system of mutual inter-dependence (along village and kin lines) and individual subordination to group norms.

The possession of land is of extreme importance in providing status and livelihood, but the system of male inheritance of land (sub-division – property divided between the children – rather than primogeniture – property inherited by the first born) results in a large number of small land-holdings which afford only a modest living. The small landholders are certainly more prosperous than landless labourers, but largely they are restricted to subsistence farming rather than more profitable cash crop production. The economic spur to migration, then, is not so much to earn a living but to supplement and build on the resources the kin group already possess. Migration is seen as an economic investment intended to raise their social and economic status in Pakistan, rather than a serious bid for a gratifying 'new life' in Britain. Consequently, the Pakistani who travelled to Britain (at least in the earlier years of post-war migration) was typically a transient rather than a permanent settler. The intention was to return eventually to Pakistan, and this signified a particular scale of values.

The concept of the 'myth of return' draws attention to the continued importance of homeland and village kin ties to the migrant. In spite of raised standards of living in Britain, many will still claim they wish to return eventually. Nevertheless, although this wish may never be fully or consciously abandoned, the implementation of the desire becomes more difficult. However, the myth has a useful function in preserving homeland values against 'Western' ideas, and it is a useful protection against the stings of racial prejudice insofar as it portrays them as no more than 'temporary hardships'.

The orientation to Pakistan is perhaps most vividly represented in the resurrection of features of that way of life within Britain. Thus, it is possible to see the migrant community attempting to carve out a life style which approximates to an extension of village life, with some necessary modifications to adjust to the new context. Of course, in the early years of migration it was not possible simply to recreate village life in Britain. Early settlers, often discharged seamen, were drawn from different villages and kin groups, yet had to share accommodation with others. So Dahya describes a 'fusion' taking place between different Pakistani groupings. Nevertheless, with the pick up in numbers generally – and more particularly with the phenomenon of sponsored migration (where the village-kin group sponsors someone to join another member in Britain) there has been a gradual process of 'fission' or internal division, first along regional then along village-kin lines. There had always been certain divisions within the Pakistani population in Britain, but over time village-kin divisions became more distinct, as larger family units were established in Britain.

Khan also points out that there are two opposing trends within the Pakistani communities: internal differentiation and solidarity. The differentiation or cleavages occur along village-kin lines, and between the more 'Western-oriented' elites and the migrants from poorer rural origins. Consequently, she argues, leadership tends to be unstable, with self-appointed 'leaders' finding it difficult to establish a wide ranging authority or credibility. Moreover, these 'leaders' are in an ambivalent position, since they are aware that their activities on behalf of the ethnic community might hinder their own 'integration' into British society. Dahya, on the other hand, argues that the ethnic entrepreneurs and community 'brokers' have a vested interest in the retention of ethnic links, since it provides a steady supply of customers for their 'ethnic' shops and services. But alongside this internal differentiation there is movement towards an over-arching solidarity among Pakistani groups. There is considerable separation between these communities and the rest of the 'host' population, and the sheer scale of racial hostility helps unite the Pakistani groups. Thus, the structured exclusion from 'white' society helps maintain the internal solidarity of these groups.

Dahya, however, departs from the usual line of depicting Pakistanis as little more than the unwitting victims of white prejudice. He questions whether racial disadvantage can simply be read off as the direct and sole result of racial prejudice and discrimination. The concentration of ethnic minorities in inferior housing in inner city areas, for example, has frequently been attributed to discrimination by urban gatekeepers (building society managers, estate agents, council housing officials) which forces the groups concerned to settle for less desirable property (cf. Rex and Moore, 1967). But Dahya restores migrants to an active position, by suggesting that they actually choose to live together in the inner city. Areas of residence are deliberately chosen because of convenience (transport routes, proximity to jobs), entrepreneurial opportunities (shops, services), and cheap accommodation (which frees money which can be sent home to sustain the homeland economy). He describes Pakistani communities as an 'army on the march' who choose to live together to defend their ethnic identity, rather than being forced into it by outside pressures.

These studies of Pakistani communities point to certain continuities between life in Pakistan and life in Britain. The 'village institutions' are resurrected within Britain, and mutual aid, pooling of resources, and religious practices are successfully perpetuated. At the same time, important changes are in process, both in Britain and in Pakistan itself. In Britain, Pakistani households tend to be smaller, the system of arranged marriages pays more respect to the wishes of the young couple, and the second generation are more visibly affected by the influence of British cultures. And when people return to Pakistan for a visit, they are sometimes surprised at the changes which have occurred in the life-styles and living standards of the 'homeland'.

(2) West Indians

The early studies of minority groups in Britain assumed that West Indians would be most likely to achieve successful integration. Their language, religious affiliations and educational system indicated their strong ties with Britain, and the first wave of migrants arrived with a firm identification with the 'mother country'. Further, their immigration was more speedily accomplished than that of the Asian groups, and soon a second generation was entering British schools and growing up with no first-hand knowledge of the Caribbean. Unfortunately, the optimistic expectations were increasingly shattered as the West Indian population suffered continuing discrimination and outright violence (e.g. in 1959 there were 'race riots' in Notting Hill and in Nottingham, where white mobs attacked West Indians). Moreover, certain observers developed the notion of an 'internal colony' to describe the disadvantaged plight of West Indian migrants in Britain. Pryce (1979), for example, argues that colonisation not only made Jamaica politically and economically dependent on Britain, but it also created a class-divided and colour-conscious society. The oppressive features of that society continued under 'neo-colonialism', when Jamaica became politically independent but remained economically weak. Pryce underlines the irony that the poor and oppressed who escape to Britain find themselves similarly trapped within British ghettos, since a system of 'internal colonialism' is formed within 'metropolitan society'. So there are clear structural parallels between life in the West Indies and in Britain, and the same unremitting pressures and blocked opportunities confront the 'have-nots'.

Hall *et al* (1978) describes the 'colony society' in the following terms:

> In another sense, the foundation of *colony society* meant the growth of internal cultural cohesiveness and solidarity within the ranks of the black population inside the corporate boundaries of the ghetto: the winning away of cultural space in which an alternative black social life could flourish. The internal colonies thus provided the material base for this cultural revival: first, of a 'West Indian consciousness', no longer simply kept alive in the head or in memory, but visible on the street; second (in the wake of the black American rebellions), of a powerful and regenerated 'black consciousness'. Here began the 'colonization' of certain streets, neighbourhoods, cafes and pubs, the growth of the revivalist churches, hymn singing and mass baptisms in the local swimming baths, the spilling out of Caribbean fruit and vegetables from the Indian shops, the shebeen and the Saturday night blues party, the construction of the sound systems, the black record shops selling blues, ska and soul – the birth of the 'native quarter' at the heart of the English city.

Hall *et al* argue that the first-generation migrants adopted a 'strategy of acceptance', a life of struggling respectability against a background of discrimination and disadvantage. However, the second generation have been less tolerant of racial injustices, and they have gradually developed a strategy of 'resistance' or 'rebellion' which has helped the growth of the cultural cohesiveness described above. Pryce, on the other hand, detected little signs of social cohesion among the black groups in his earlier Bristol study and he gives much more attention to the diversity of life-styles within the ghetto. One of the more interesting examples of this diversity is Rastafarianism, which was not yet prominent in the late 1960s when Pryce began his fieldwork. However, this movement has been intensively studied by Cashmore (1979), and it is worth looking at his study in greater detail.

There was a marked upsurge in the popularity of Rastafarian ideas and lifestyles among young British blacks in the 1970s. They were easily identifiable by their rolled, uncut hair (dreadlocks) and the Ethiopian colours of red, gold and green. The reggae music of Bob Marley and others created a positive public awareness of their existence, but they also attracted a controversial reputation for drug-taking and criminal activities, a reputation which Cashmore shows is unwarranted. Cashmore's stated intention was to 'uncover the social foundations of a particular conception of reality', and this involved him in constructing the 'conceptual maps' of Rastafarians, highlighting their motivations, dispositions and cognitive states. This was, to say the least, a methodologically difficult task, and Cashmore frankly concedes that he relied heavily on 'intuition and inference'. At the same time, however, he researched the historical and material reality within which these subjective states were formed and sustained.

Cashmore claims that the 'movement' is an extension of a Jamaican historical tradition in which political objectives are couched in visions of redemption and supernatural transformations of the world. This tradition blurs the dividing lines between secular and religious objectives, and between the supernatural and the 'everyday' world. A particularly important period in this tradition came in the 1920s and 1930s with the writings of Marcus Garvey, in which he argued against 'integration' and depicted Africa as the spiritual homeland and eventual destination of blacks throughout the world. Although Garvey enjoyed a rather chequered political career, his prophecy (that the crowning of a black king in Africa would herald a new dawn) was seized upon and developed after the assumption to power of Haile Selassie as Emperor of Ethiopia in 1930. But what is surprising is how this somewhat distinct and esoteric cult came to be developed creatively by young Black Britons in the 1970s. Cashmore suggests six factors favourable to development of this kind of ethnicity.

(1) Concentration of a frustrated black population in urban areas.

(2) The unfulfilled aspirations and general disillusionment of this

population made them very receptive to new ideas which suggested some sort of solution to their disaffection.

(3) A cultural apparatus which percolated Rastafarian ideas through the popular and widely available medium of music.

(4) The survival of a gang structure from the 1960s – the remnants of the urban 'rude boy' culture common in downtown areas of Jamaica, and which had existed for a while alongside skinhead culture in Britain in the 1960s. This provided a vehicle for the transmission of ideas.

(5) Rising self-awareness and a sharpened political sense among blacks, who were less convinced by integrationist promises.

(6) Gradual state of 'drift' which loosened the ties to the dominant moral order, including the culture of their parents. This heightened the socialising influence of the street peer group.

Cashmore describes a 'kaleidoscopic array of beliefs and ideas', but the central concept which assists in forming 'boundaries' to the movement is that of Babylon. This concept refers to the whole structure and ideology of white oppression of blacks, originating with imperialism. Not only were blacks abused in physical ways (slavery and ill-treatment) but the whites spread an ideology which perpetuated black subordination and created a lingering sense of inferiority among blacks themselves. Christianity, for example, seemed to preach that blacks should remain meek and mild because they would thus reap their ultimate reward in heaven. So blacks have to purge 'internal' sources of oppression as well as external ones if they are to achieve freedom. This involves finding the 'true self' which can be explored through biblical guidance. The notion of 'brotherhood', however, emphasises that blacks are ultimately united in their common struggle, rather than seeking individual salvation. Indeed they are joined by the belief that God (Jah) resides within every one of them.

Cashmore presents a defence for some of the aspects of Rasta culture which have been most often criticised. Feminists, for example, have condemned the subordinate status of Rasta women ('queens'). Against this, Cashmore argues that one of the main tasks of the movement is to elevate and raise the status of black manhood, which has been severely undermined by the 'matrifocal' emphasis within black culture. Moreover, although Rastas do not marry (marriage is regarded as sinful), Rastafarians claim that their sexual relations are characterised by respect and honour, which they sharply contrast to the decadence and exploitation of 'Western' culture.

Another criticism levelled by radicals is that the Rasta culture is essentially escapist: the message seems to be to stand back and let Babylon crumble from its own corruption. Some radicals have interpreted it as a form of rebellion which has lost its way, taking a 'quietist' route. And certainly Cashmore points out that most of the 'members' are drawn from the lower ranks of the working class, those who presumably should be in the forefront of rebellion. But Cashmore insists that it is not simply an instrumental movement seeking material advantage. Rather, it pays serious attention to the need for identity and culture as well. There is a 'quantum leap' between a solely secular political movement and that of Rastafarianism, which blends secular and religious viewpoints within one world view. Thus, it does not fit neatly into radical accounts of 'protest' groups. Here is how Rex and Tomlinson (1979) sum up its contribution:

> Black youth are in need of a philosophy and a culture which gives them an identity and self-respect in contrast with the degraded self-image which white society imposes on them. This was what, first, Black Islam, and then the Black Power movement did for the ghettoized descendants of slaves in the USA. The blacks of contemporary Britain are also the descendants of slaves deprived of a culture, even if they have not experienced the degradation of the ghetto to the same extent as the American blacks. It looks as though Rastafari in its British growth and development will provide them at least with the beginnings of a culture of self respect ... it is probably the most important single fact about West Indian society and culture in Britain.

Ethnicity: A Critique

The preceding ethnographies by no means exhaust the entire repertoire of available studies, but they do illustrate the general direction and familiar preoccupations of this approach. In turning to some of the critical debates surrounding ethnic studies, our discussion will be organised around two issues, their *descriptive accuracy* and their *explanatory value*.

(A) Ethnicity as Description

There are great methodological problems in 'reading' a culture accurately, and this leaves a wide latitude for descriptive errors and intruding value-judgements. So it is perhaps not surprising that students of ethnicity themselves disagree on most of the following issues:

(1) How 'different' are ethnic cultures? Plainly, these differences are sometimes clear-cut (as in the case of religious belief-systems), but more frequently they involve subtle variations in emphasis, and in many essentials the ethnic minorities subscribe to the same values as the majority culture. It is worth noting, for instance, that some recent research (Field, 1984) arrived at the conclusion that the attitudes of 'blacks' and 'Asians' living in Britain are not dramatically different from those of their white counterparts. Some commentators even suggest that such an apparently 'divergent' movement as Rastafarianism is more correctly viewed as a case of 'symbolic ethnicity' (Gans, 1979), a matter of cultural fashion and stylised identity which does not bite too deeply into the lives of its 'followers'. Rather than indicating an all-consuming commitment to 'alternative' values, the popularity of Rastafarianism, is sometimes based on the relatively casual matter of surface style. And this is only one of the problems of interpretation confronting ethnic researchers. It soon becomes obvious that these researchers face the difficult task of striking the correct balance, one which gives due weight to cultural variations without at the same time exaggerating the gap which exists between the various ethnic minority cultures, and between them and the rather under-researched 'host' culture (or, more appropriately, host *cultures*).

(2) How problem-ridden are ethnic cultures? Accusations of ethnocentrism are frequently hurled at writers on ethnicity, and one of the most heated debates concerns the position of the 'matrifocal' family structure in West Indian culture. Critics argue that not only has the frequency of single-parent, female-headed family units been grossly exaggerated, but researchers have been blinded by their own cultural values and have wrongly interpreted this type of family structure as 'weak', 'pathological', and 'inadequate'. This overlooks the need for cultural relativism (does it seem a problem to the people concerned?) and it underestimates the strengths of West Indian family life. In addition to charges of ethnocentrism, it is frequently alleged that sexist assumptions creep into the descriptions of Asian females. Thus, a distorted stereotype of 'passive' Asian females is circulated, in which they are portrayed as 'subjugated' and 'oppressed' by patriarchal Asian culture. Parmar (1982) argues that this patronising over-simplification ignores the brave and constructive role played by Asian women in resisting racism, capitalism, and patriarchy. These criticisms of ethnic studies certainly deserve attention, but it is also important to note that mainstream ethnicity writers do not always agree on these descriptions and evaluations. Moreover, not all the researchers are white (Pryce is Jamaican) or male (Parmar is just as scathing about white feminists). And it would be curious if ethnic cultures contained no 'internal' problems, tensions or weaknesses, especially given the damaging history of racism and the dislocating impact of migration.

(3) **Is there a 'generation' gap in ethnic cultures?** A recurrent topic of interest in ethnic research is the changing nature of cultural attachments over time, and so a great deal of attention has been paid to the second generation. Do they faithfully preserve the cultural heritage of the first generation or do they break loose from this tradition? It is commonly argued that first-generation West Indian migrants were typically 'compliant' and 'assimilationist' in orientation, whereas the second-generation are more truculent, alienated and militant. Indeed, the youngsters are portrayed as 're-discovering' elements of black history (Rastafarianism, Black Power) and creatively developing them in ways disapproved of by the first-generation. Likewise, Asian youth are sometimes depicted as bridling at customs like arranged marriages, and as flirting with 'Western' values and behaviour in a way which suggests a slow movement away from the culture of the first-generation. However, writers differ as to the extent of the culture gap between the first and second generations, and on whether this is indeed a 'culture gap' or simply an 'age' gap which becomes less marked as youth grow older.

Of course, these disagreements and criticisms do not constitute objections in principle to the ethnic approach. They simply point to the difficulties of cultural analysis and the margin for mis-interpretation. Nevertheless, there still remains the problem of determining the explanatory value of ethnic research: is the approach confined to the cataloguing of 'exotic' cultural differences, or does it have real theoretical significance?

(B) Ethnicity as Explanation

We will focus on two main questions in this section:

(1) Why do people cultivate allegiance to ethnic groups?

(2) What explanatory value has 'culture' for an understanding of race relations?

(1) **The sources of ethnicity.** Part of the theoretical problem consists in explaining why ethnic groups achieve prominence in the first place. McKay (1982) identifies two opposing schools of explanation for the importance of ethnic groups in modern industrialised societies: the

'*primordialist*' and the '*mobilisationist*' arguments. Primordialists contend that the strength of ethnicity derives from the way it meets the human need for deep-seated, sacred, non-contractual attachments. Ethnic allegiances answer our 'natural' need for belonging and community, and so ethnic groups emerge spontaneously from the innermost recesses of human nature. A more technical version of primordialism is afforded by 'sociobiology' (van den Berghe, 1978) which suggests that ethnic or racial attachments are coded in the genes. Ethnicity is explained in sociobiology as a particular example of 'kin selection', or the tendency to show favouritism to people of similar appearance or kin networks, in order that the common genes have a better chance of evolutionary survival.

The 'mobilisationist' school, on the other hand, suggests that ethnic loyalties are peripheral rather than primordial, and so groups only mobilise ethnic symbols when it offers them some strategic advantage in obtaining access to social, political or economic resources. In the British context, these mobilisationist arguments are usually translated into the concept of 'reactive ethnicity', which conveys the tendency for ethnic group members to construct ethnicity as a defence against racism and discrimination. Thus, Ballard and Ballard (1977) describe the ethnic ties of first-generation Sikhs as little more than a somewhat muted expression of their cultural traditions; the second-generation, however, attempted to strike compromises with British society, but were stung into 'reactive' pride in ethnicity because of the continuing experience of repeated rebuffs and racist humiliations. Moreover, this victimisation created a greater awareness of the similar problems faced by other ethnic groups, and so the second generation are increasingly reaching beyond the more parochial loyalties of their predecessors to embrace a more over-arching pan-Asian identity. As members of single ethnic groups or cross-alliances, the members manipulate ethnic symbols to build a positive identity and to engage in political and economic activity to promote their material interests.

These mobilisationist views helpfully avoid the rather mystical and circular arguments of the primordialist approach, and they appear more useful in understanding the ebb and flow of ethnic loyalties. However, it is not always clear what particular 'interests' are being promoted or defended. If the interests involved are not just material, but include identity, then this merely seems to take us back to primordial arguments. Also, just how strong are the tendencies to 'race' (or 'black' or 'Asian') alliances in comparison with specific 'ethnic' ties or even broad 'class' groupings? How much is the stress on ethnicity due to 'reaction', and how much to a more straightforward 'choice' to follow cultural traditions? Ethnicity obviously involves both 'emotional' and 'strategic' factors, and it would be premature to claim that these questions have been resolved.

(2) Cultural explanations. 'Radicals' of various persuasions have been extremely unhappy about the heavy reliance of ethnicity studies on 'culture' as a key to understanding race-related issues. They argue that the logical consequence of ethnicity studies is to attach ultimate 'blame' to the ethnic minorities themselves. Attention is almost exclusively focussed on the 'migrants' and their cultural peculiarities, and heavy emphasis is typically placed on 'pathological' or 'inappropriate' features of these cultures. It is only a short step, then, to 'blaming the victim': crime among West Indian groups is attributed to their 'weak' family structures or 'macho' cultures rather than to the economic deprivations created by capitalist processes; the disadvantaged economic position of Asian women is seen as resulting from their culturally-approved 'subordinate' role rather than from the exploitation of cheap labour in Britain. The predominant emphasis on cultural minorities conveniently deflects attention away from the cultural racism of the 'hosts' and the institutional racism of British society. 'Race' problems are subsequently framed in terms of 'mutual misunderstandings' and the solutions are posited along the tame lines of 'multi-cultural education' and 'cultural pluralism'. Bourne (1983) bitterly attacks ethnicity theorists as little more than 'cheerleaders' for cultural diversity who thereby absolve themselves from combatting the racism endemic in capitalist society. For the radicals, the underlying problems are structural ones of power and conflict, and these issues cannot be tackled by abstract debates about 'culture'. Racial disadvantage, they argue, is not the 'natural' outcome of a multicultural society in which some ethnic groups cling to inappropriate values: it is the structural outcome of an exploitative, oppressive society which can only be transformed through radical change.

In their eagerness to make political points, the radical critics have undoubtedly caricatured ethnic studies, and it is arguable that not all ethnographers are quite so naïve or politically insensitive as the critics make out. Few writers lay heavy stress on the 'pathology' of ethnic cultures, and if 'weakness' or 'inadequacy' are highlighted it is usually against a background of structural strain (cf. Pryce). Clearly, the issues of culture conflict and cultural misunderstandings cannot be ducked in a society in which the notion of an 'alien wedge' destroying 'British culture' is so politically entrenched, and so we should be grateful to ethnicity theorists for pursuing these matters. Moreover, the emphasis on ethnicity has had the welcome effect of restoring the ethnic minorities to the position of 'active subjects', fully human beings with their own aspirations, allegiances and consciousness. If nothing else, ethnicity studies have successfully challenged the notion of migrants as mere empty vessels or passive victims without a history and a consciousness of their own. Of course, this emphasis becomes dangerous if it is assumed that there is some permanent cultural 'essence' attached to ethnic groups, such that they will behave in the same manner regardless of circumstances. As Ballard and Ballard point out, we cannot assume that minority group behaviour is the direct expression of internal cultural preferences, but neither is it a direct reaction to external, objective constraints (material deprivation, prejudice, etc.):

> It should be recognized that the external constraints, such as the migrant's position in the labour and housing markets, or the discrimination he faces, are ultimately prior to the internal preferences of the group... It is the external constraints of discrimination which set the limits within which South Asians and West Indians in Britain may operate. *But the particular behaviour of different groups may only be finally explained in terms of the culturally determined choices made within these limits as well as the various ethnic strategies used to counteract, circumvent or overthrow those constraints.* (R. and C. Ballard, 1977)

So always we have to examine the interplay between 'cultural' and 'structural' factors. In the next chapter we introduce the 'structural' accounts of race relations.

Chapter Five

Structure and Conflict

The broad contours of racism in Britain were sketched out in an earlier chapter, where it was argued that 'coloured' people suffer from various forms of social disadvantage (institutional racism) and endure continuing problems of racial prejudice (cultural racism) and discrimination (racialism). These three inter-linked elements of racism form a complex and shifting reality, but nevertheless the available evidence consistently suggests the presence of significant racial tensions and structured racial inequalities in modern Britain. It is now time to move beyond the mere documentation of racism towards a search for its major causes. Why does 'race' acquire such a loaded social significance that it leads to the victimisation of black people and the sharp limitation of their life-chances? Why do exclusion boundaries tend to form around socially-defined racial groups? The main concern of this chapter is with 'structural' explanations of racism, and especially those versions which lay stress on deep social conflicts. The discussion is centred round two important topics: the relationship between 'race' and stratification systems, and the role of racist ideologies.

Race and Stratification

The sociological literature on race relations makes frequent reference to the location of racial minorities within stratification systems, and conflict models especially are inclined to regard the class structure as having a crucial influence on race issues. This is particularly true of the various Marxist accounts of racism in Britain, and indeed sometimes 'racial' groups disappear entirely from the analysis as they are submerged in a more general discussion of class conflict. Apart from the Marxist accounts, there are also studies which follow in the tradition of Weber, and Rex is the most prominent representative of this kind of approach. Although the Weberian approach is sometimes described as 'reformist', and although it rejects the Marxist notion of a historical class struggle fought to a revolutionary conclusion, it has more in common with the 'conflict' school than with functionalism. Some of the differences between these Marxist and Weberian approaches can be highlighted by looking at the work of Castles and Kosack on the one hand, and Rex and Moore on the other.

(1) **Castles and Kosack** (1973). These writers approach race relations from a Marxist standpoint, and emphasis is placed upon class conflict within capitalism. Capitalism is described as driven by a relentless search for profits, and in this search it has created a situation of under-development in ex-colonies (West Indian islands, India, Algeria, etc.). Moreover, the uneven development of capitalism has led to a split in Europe between the prosperous 'metropolis' countries like France, Germany and Britain, and the more backward areas like Turkey, Yugoslavia and Greece. These less developed nations – the ex-colonies and the poorer European countries – offer convenient reserves of cheap labour which can be drawn upon when the metropolis centres have labour shortages, and this is precisely what has happened in the post-war period of economic expansion. The prosperous capitalist countries of Western Europe enjoyed better living conditions and improved occupational mobility opportunities, and so the native population deserted the low-status, low-wage menial jobs, thereby creating a labour shortage which was solved by drawing migrants from the less developed countries. The migrants constitute a 'replacement population' filling the undesirable but essential jobs vacated by the indigenous population, and so they settle in the lower ranks of the working class.

It is their emphasis on the labour needs of capitalism which encourages Castles and Kosack to insist that there is no clear division between New Commonwealth migrants to Britain and the European or Arab 'guestworkers' in Germany and France. Admittedly, the legal and civil rights of the guestworkers are more precarious, and they are less likely to be accompanied by their families, but basically they fill the same economic role. Consequently, Castles and Kosack decide to break away from mainstream race relations approaches and they abandon ethnic and phenotypical considerations in favour of an emphasis upon class position. Furthermore, they break away from the cruder versions of the immigrant-host model which portray a rather homogeneous host society, and underline instead the class-divided nature of the receiving societies: 'Western European societies are class societies based on the ownership and control of the means of production by a small minority, and on the concomitant domination and exploitation of the masses. Social relationships are characterised not by harmony and free will, but by conflict and coercion'. The migrants, therefore, arrive into an hierarchical social order which is understood in terms of the Marxist distinction between two main classes, the bourgeoisie and the proletariat. Nevertheless, the migrants do not simply enter a class society: they also have an impact upon it. Castles and Kosack admit that the evidence on the long-term effects of migrant labour is sketchy, but they speculate on possible consequences. Most importantly, they believe the migrants create an internal split within the working class, even though the long-term interests of the native working class and the migrants coincide. The basic insecurity of the native working class makes them prey to racism, and they see the migrants as a threat rather than potential allies in a common struggle against capitalist exploiters. This split is both objective (in terms of the different kinds of jobs allocated to the two groups) and subjective (migrants have lower social status, and are the victims of prejudice), and it hinders the development of class consciousness.

Basically, then, Castles and Kosack explore the system needs of capitalism, the influence this has on migration patterns, and the consequences of this migration on the receiving societies (where capitalists benefit from cheap labour) and the sending societies (which are drained of talent). In swinging the debate away from familiar race relations preoccupations towards economic and class categories, they have been accused of explaining everything in terms of the economic base, and it is certainly true that they underestimate the importance of ethnicity. However, they do allow that political and cultural factors are important: for example, they argue that the increasingly restrictive immigration legislation in Britain was determined not by the economic interests of capitalists (who benefit from a large 'reserve army of labour'), but by wider political processes and cultural debates (e.g. in mass media).

The approach of Castles and Kosack has the virtue of setting British race issues against a historical backcloth and within a global context of political and economic relationships between nations. Of course, there are important differences between 'liberals' and 'Marxists' on the nature and consequences of these connections. Liberals usually admit that colonialism involved conflict and exploitation, but they also stress the beneficial consequences, especially the ways in which the more industrialised nations have assisted in the 'modernisation' of less developed countries. Modernisation theories (Hoogvelt, 1976) assume that 'development' is represented by the types of technology and social organisation which exist in Western countries. Overall, the influence of the Western countries has been to encourage the colonies and ex-colonies to overcome all those 'obstacles' (social, cultural and techno-logical) which prevented their development, and in this respect they have set a useful example to the less favoured nations. Some branches of 'classical' Marxism also believe that the capitalist countries had a 'progressive' role to play in dragging peasant societies out of their stagnation and setting them on the road to capitalist development and the eventual socialist revolution. But some neo-Marxists (e.g. Frank, 1967) argue that, instead of generating capitalist development in these countries, the major powers have imposed 'dependency' or 'under-development'. This notion is captured by Harrison (1979):

> Colonial powers laid the foundation of the present division of the world into industrial nations on the one hand, and hewers of wood and drawers of water on the other. They wiped out indigenous industry and forced the colonies to buy their manufactures. They undermined the self-sufficiency of the Third World and transformed it into a source of raw materials for western industry ... In this way the colonial powers created the world economic order that still prevails today, of industrial centre and primary-producing periphery, prosperous metropolis and poverty-stricken satellites.

Whatever their particular disagreements, both 'modernisation' and 'dependency' theorists agree that a large gulf still separates the metropolis and satellite countries.

(2) Rex and Moore. In the course of their field study of Sparkbrook in Birmingham in the mid-1960s, Rex and Moore (1967) argued that much racial conflict can be understood by examining basic urban processes and problems, and the key urban process they highlight is that of competition for scarce yet desired housing. Whereas Marxists identify two main classes in terms of relationship to the means of production, Rex and Moore adopt a more flexible Weberian position which defines a variety of classes according to given 'market situations', and they point out that one such market is housing. This leads them to coin the notion of 'housing classes' to designate groups which occupy varying positions of strength in the housing market and system of housing allocation. These housing classes do not coincide with the Marxist classes (although there is some relationship between them), since one Marxist class would consist of several housing classes characterised by different interests and market situations. Another typical Weberian emphasis is their desire to develop analyses of the 'subjective' aspects of class situations, necessitating an exploration of popular world-views, including the ways in which people define their own class membership. Although there is no rigid consensus of values, Rex and Moore suspect that nearly everyone aspires to the 'suburban ideal' of 'relatively detached family life'. Nevertheless, the competitive class struggle for this kind of privately-owned, detached or semi-detached suburban housing creates winners and losers, and the less powerful classes have to settle for less desirable housing (flats, terraces), tenure systems (council or private tenancies) or areas of residence (slums, inner-city areas, problem estates).

Rex and Moore acknowledge both the depressed economic situation in the ex-colonies and the economic motives which inspire migration, and they are also sensitive to the continuing bonds between migrants and their countries of origin. But the main focus of the Sparkbrook study was an investigation of the disadvantaged position of New Commonwealth immigrants in the housing market. As far as the 'private' sector of house purchase is concerned, they faced various problems: usually their incomes were low and their savings modest, and in addition they experienced discrimination by vendors, estate agents and building society officials. In the 'council' sector they were confronted by unrealistic residence requirements and long waiting lists which overlooked the special circumstances of their recent arrival; and when they did qualify for council tenure, they were frequently given inferior accommodation on the basis of housing visitor reports which embodied public prejudices. The only solution for many immigrants, therefore, was to gravitate towards old, large and decaying property in inner-city twilight areas like Sparkbrook. These unattractive houses were purchased by communal pooling of resources or by high-interest, short term loans from banks and finance companies (since building societies were cautious about lending money for short-lease property). Generally this put serious financial strain on the migrants, and this accounts for the high proportion of multi-occupation and sub-letting: in order to maintain repayments, the purchaser was forced to take in lodgers, many of whom were fellow migrants unable to obtain alternative accommodation. Unfortunately, these areas of settlement usually suffer from various manifestations of urban deterioration, and it is against this background of decay that racial hostilities are intensified. White residents blame the immigrants for 'creating' the general housing problems, the migrants are resented for altering the 'character' of the area, and racist stereotypes enjoy wide circulation.

However, Rex and Moore argue that it is the discriminatory policies and inadequate housing provision which cause concentrated settlements of migrants, and they show that the migrants are little more than scapegoats for wider social ills.

The Sparkbrook study was enormously influential in directing attention to insitutional practices and policy inadequacies which magnify racial tensions, and it served as a useful catalyst for interesting debates on race issues. But a number of the particular details of urban patterns and processes were questioned, and Rex later admitted that Sparkbrook was an untypical area (e.g. in areas like Handsworth, also in Birmingham, single-family owner-occupation was more common among New Commonwealth migrants). Moreover, the notion of 'housing classes' was subjected to fairly rigorous analytical challenge from some quarters, and it was even suggested that the basic arguments could be accepted without the necessity of devising new 'classes'. Also some 'ethnicity' theorists claimed that migrants actively sought out inner-city areas (in order to retain ethnic ties and to exploit the greater entrepreneurial opportunities these areas afforded) rather than being forced into them because of discrimination or financial necessity. But perhaps the most pressing issue concerns the extent to which housing and environmental conflicts are responsible for racial tensions.

In a later work, Rex (1978) states that housing conflicts are only one source of racism, and he is not at all hopeful that mere urban improvement in itself will remedy matters. There are many reasons for racism – the colonial legacy, class conflict, widespread fear and insecurity – and the full citizenship of black people will require a concentrated effort to resolve the deep-seated problems of British society.

The Underclass

It is one thing to claim that racial conflict is largely a derivative of class conflict, but it still remains a perplexing task to specify precisely how racial groups fit into stratification systems. Various 'extreme' conceptualisations have been offered, including the notion of a 'plural society' (where racial or ethnic groups of more or less equal ranking lead separate existences, mixing only for limited economic purposes) and the 'colour-caste model' (where black and white groups are both stratified internally along class lines, but a rather rigid caste-like barrier between them symbolises and maintains the superior status of whites). In Britain, however, most of the analyses have related racial groups to conventional Marxist and Weberian categories. Nevertheless, even within these traditions there is plenty of disagreement. Miles (1982) helps structure the relevant debates by identifying some dominant stances:

(1) Unitary Working Class. Westergaard and Resler (1976) contend that too much attention has been paid to the special problems created by racial discrimination. Coloured people and the white working class share the same basic relation to the means of production, and it is this common class membership which oppresses them: 'Preoccupied with the disabilities that attach to colour, liberal reformers and research workers have been busy rediscovering what in fact are common disabilities of class: widespread and long-standing conditions inherent in the workings of capital, market and state in a divided society'.

(2) Divided Working Class. Castles and Kosack, as we have already seen, also work largely within a two-class model (bourgeoisie and proletariat), but unlike the previous authors they believe that black migration has created an objective and subjective split within the working class: 'In objective terms, immigrant workers belong to the working class. But within this class they form a bottom stratum, due to the subordinate status of their occupations'.

(3) Underclass Thesis. Rex and Tomlinson (1979) use the term underclass to signify a disadvantaged group which does not share the same experiences or privileges as the white working class. In their Handsworth study they found a 'structural break' between the white working class and the coloured underclass in a range of market situations (employment, housing and education), and of course racial discrimination is another distinguishing factor. They describe coloured people as leading a 'marginalised' existence since they have not yet been fully incorporated into traditional working class organisations (such as trade unions and the Labour Party).

(4) 'Racialised' Class Fraction. Miles accepts the broad distinction between bourgeoisie and proletariat, but he emphasises the existence of different 'fractions' or sectional interest groups within each. So the working class is not 'unitary' and it is not simply 'divided' into two main camps. As for the 'underclass' thesis, Miles insists that this exaggerates the disadvantage suffered by black groups, and it places too much emphasis on racial discrimination rather than class dynamics. In Miles' conceptualisation, therefore, black people appear at different class levels (mainly within working class, but also in middle class groups) but always as a distinctive fraction which has been 'racialised' (endowed with overtones of racial inferiority).

It is exceedingly difficult to choose between these apparently rival views on the position of racial minorities within the British class system. Although there is agreement that coloured people are over-represented in the lower reaches of the stratification system, it is also clear that they are not exclusively confined to those zones, and this makes the articulation of precise lines of division a daunting task. In order to explore these problems further, it is instructive to take a closer look at the 'underclass' notion.

The notion of an underclass was first developed in the United States, where it was used to refer to that section of the population which seemed permanently trapped in a situation of poverty and unemployment. Although the term is not necessarily confined to black people, it had particular relevance to those people living in the black ghettoes like Watts, which erupted into violence and riots in the 1960s. Briefly, the sense of hopelessness and despair in these ghettoes was transformed into desperate action and protest, a dramatic expression of their feelings of marginality. Likewise, some British commentators (Young and Lea, 1982) have described the 'marginalisation' of black people as a major factor behind the British 'race riots' of the 1980s. Young and Lea suggest that the black population has been squeezed to the very margins of society, and this has denied them the normal channels for resolving their grievances. Unlike the white working class, they are distanced from traditional trade union and political party activity.

This theme of marginalisation is pursued also in Rex and Tomlinson's study of Handsworth. What Rex and Tomlinson argue is that there has not been any marked sense in which ethnic minorities have gained access to those key political, educational, economic and cultural institutions which would enable them to compete on equal terms with whites. Despite their characteristic working-class employment profile, it does not make sense to describe ethnic minorities as part of the working class; rather, they constitute an underclass. Rex and Tomlinson allow that the concept of 'underclass' does not imply that everyone within it is unemployed, but they do point out that ethnic minorities are subject to higher unemployment rates. Some evidence for this is supplied by the 1981 *Labour Force Survey* (see table overleaf).

However, the distinctiveness of the 'underclass' position persists even for those who are employed, and this distinctiveness is captured in the idea of a *'dual labour market'*. A dual labour market is one which shows clear divisions between two employment groups: the primary market (characterised by high pay, security of employment, and good training and promotion prospects) and the secondary market (characterised by low pay, insecurity of employment, and few opportunities for training or promotion). The expectation is that the

Ethnic Groups: Economic status of adults, percentages

Males	White	West Indian	Asian	Other	All
Self-employed	9	4	14	8	9
Employees	61	65	55	50	60
Out of employment	8	19	15	10	10
Economically inactive	22	12	17	32	22
Females					
Self-employed	2	1	3	3	2
Employed	40	56	30	38	40
Out of employment	4	11	7	7	5
Economically inactive	53	32	60	53	53

(Source: *Social Trends*, 1983)
[Reproduced with the permission of the Controller of Her Majesty's Stationery Office]

underclass are highly concentrated in the secondary market, and this creates a vicious circle: the stigmatised racial minority can only land jobs in the secondary market; and their over-representation in this market serves to reinforce their inferior social status. Again, the *Labour Force Survey* gives some indication of this pattern of under-representation in the more desirable jobs.

Ethnic Groups: People in employment by sex and socio-economic group, percentages.

Males	White	West Indian	Asian	Other	All
Professional, employers, managers	22	6	20	24	22
Intermediate and junior non manual	18	7	14	23	18
Skilled manual and non professional	38	49	35	27	38
Semi-skilled and unskilled	21	38	31	24	21
Females					
Professional, employers, managers	8	2	7	5	7
Intermediate and junior non manual	53	50	41	52	52
Skilled manual	7	4	13	8	7
Semi-unskilled	31	42	38	34	32

(Source: *Social Trends*, 1983)
[Reproduced with the permission of the Controller of Her Majesty's Stationery Office]

However, this table also indicates that ethnic minorities are not exclusively concentrated in the lower reaches of the occupational hierarchy and so this creates some difficulty in establishing whether they are truly an underclass. Rex and Tomlinson certainly recognise this spread over the occupational range, and they even allow that Asians in Britain may have a 'Jewish' future (where they prosper but remain separate from the rest of the population). But they insist on the notion of an underclass because of the *predominance* of ethnic groups in shift work, in low status occupations and in dirty industries. Nevertheless, the admitted spread of occupations poses problems for the underclass model. As Braham (1980) states, 'To say that skin colour involves a number of disadvantages is not to say that all black people occupy the same position in the labour market, and to establish that black workers are concentrated in less skilled jobs is not to establish the existence of a black "underclass".' And this lack of a clear 'structural break' between whites and blacks is one of the reasons why the 'unitary working class model' and the 'racialised class fraction' model depart from the underclass thesis. Some of the disagreements also stem from the basic ambiguity surrounding the meaning of the term 'underclass'. However, these disagreements also relate to the political strategies which black groups might adopt. Marxists tend to favour the 'unitary' and 'divided' conceptions, because they believe that whites and blacks should join forces in the class struggle. But the Weberian notion of underclass is less convinced of the unity of interests and revolutionary potential of the working class. Thus, Rex and Tomlinson believe that separate ethnic organisations and political activities are a fruitful means of furthering the special interests of the ethnic groups concerned, at least until they gain full entry into the dominant institutions of society. They also argue that the major political parties should call a truce over race issues and develop a high-profile strategy to overcome racial disadvantage. Multi-cultural education, housing and employment policies, and anti-discrimination measures are needed to rectify the plight of the underclass. As a Weberian, Rex places his trust in reform rather than revolution, but it must also be said that he remains rather pessimistic about the prospects for improvement. In spite of his belief that ethnic groups should engage in 'effective political organisation on their own behalf', he realises that the 'deterministic belief system' of racism severely limits their opportunities.

Racism as Capitalist Ideology

One of the chief preoccupations of the Marxist treatment of race issues concerns the nature, origins and functions of misleading racist ideologies. An ideology is a set of beliefs, ideas and values which has a recognisable shape and an organising cluster of recurrent themes. Sometimes the ideology is articulated in the form of systematic theoretical and philosophical statements, but it also appears at the more inconsistent level of 'commonsense' or 'folk wisdom'; so racist ideologies are represented in pseudo-scientific theories ('biological determinism') in media portrayals and in 'street-level' myths and rumours about disreputable habits of coloured people. Miles (1982) suggests that the defining feature of racist ideology – or 'racism', as he prefers – is that it ascribes negatively-evaluated characteristics in a deterministic manner to a group which is additionally identified as being in some way biologically distinct. Several examples of these racist beliefs and stereotypes have already been reviewed in earlier chapters, so the main focus in this section is on the origins and functions of racism.

Marxists take issue with those explanations of racism which stress universal moral failures (selfishness, cruelty) or narrow psychological causes (misperceptions, personality disorders), and argue instead that racism is rooted in historical and material situations of struggle and conflict. More specifically, the source of racist ideologies is traced to the emergence of capitalism and its process of world-wide expansion. Cox (1970) even speculates: 'It is possible that without capitalism, a chance occurrence among whites, the world might never have experienced race prejudice'. The exploitative processes of colonial expansion (the Iberian conquest of South America, British penetration of India, the European scramble for African territory) are therefore portrayed as the fertile seedbed of racism, both creating and transforming the nature of inter-racial relationships and concurrently spawning racist beliefs. Now, many liberals would agree that colonialism had a profound influence on race relations, but they tend to locate the conflicts in the past and view current race problems as resulting from the unfortunate cultural legacy which has been handed down from those years. But the distinctive thrust of Marxist theories is the claim that the production relations of capitalism harbour the conflicts and tensions which create the 'necessity' of racism. And, since capitalism still predominates in the West, its inherent (but shifting) contradictions continue to fuel racist sentiments in various ways. Consequently, a Marxist approach addresses not just the initial 'production' of racism by the capitalist system, but also the ways in which racist ideologies are 'reproduced' and progressively transformed as capitalism itself alters and encounters new problems. And the key to the lasting connection between 'capitalism' and 'racism' is located in the important functions which racism serves for the perpetuation of the capitalist system. These functions can be grouped around three headings: legitimisation, divide-and-rule, and scapegoating.

(1) Legitimisation. Colonial conquests were carried out by supposedly 'civilised', 'Christian' nations which were ultimately obliged to justify and legitimate their actions. The doctrine of racial superiority was a very convenient device for this purpose, allowing the subjugation and exploitation of the colonised to appear somehow natural, pre-ordained and even in the long-term interests of those who were subjugated. So it can be argued that racism serves as a powerful rationalisation for questionable practices, and it also protects privileged or ruling groups from damaging criticism by putting a gloss on exploitation or callous neglect. The social deprivations of blacks in present-day Britain, for example, may be attributed – via racist stereo-types – to their alleged innate inferiority rather than to any serious defects or injustices in the social order.

(2) Divide and Rule. The prevalence of racist beliefs drives a wedge between white and black workers, and this creates a divided working class which is thereby weakened in the struggle against employers. Indeed, this wedge may be deliberately encouraged by employers who can use it to manipulate the work-force to keep wages low. After the Emancipation of slaves in the southern USA, for example, some unscrupulous plantation owners employed agitators to stir up friction between blacks and whites, and this allowed them to play off one group against the other.

(3) Scapegoating. Racism encourages a scapegoating process in which the inherent frustrations and tensions of capitalism are allowed a 'safe' outlet by being directed at a visible and relatively vulnerable target group – blacks – rather than being directed back to the basic structure of capitalism. This scapegoating process allows a temporary release of pent-up strains and frustrations among the white population, and it deflects attention away from the serious crises of capitalism. Housing shortages are then blamed on an influx of alien immigrants rather than on the normal processes of an unjust housing market; unemployment is blamed on aliens taking all the jobs rather than on the crisis of profitability within capitalism.

These 'functions' help to underline the point that ideologies have real and important effects on the economic and political life of a country, and this is why Marxists sometimes represent racism as a set of 'practices' which exert a definite influence on the ideological, political and economic 'levels' of society. But always the emphasis is on the economic forces which generate and sustain these ideologies.

Policing the Crisis

One of the most illuminating accounts of these functions is the study by Hall *et al* (1978) who offer an interesting and immensely detailed version of the scapegoat argument. Their starting point is the debate about 'mugging' in Britain, a debate which became more and more prominent in the early 1970s after some heavily-publicised cases. Curiously, the mugging scare did not seem justified in terms of an unprecedented rise in the relevant crime figures, and so they used the notion of a 'moral panic' to draw attention to the exaggerated nature of the fears and rumours surrounding the issue. Moreover, a central feature of the debate was the close identification of mugging with blacks, an identification which seemed 'natural' and 'reasonable' in light of some familiarity with the crime debates in the United States. Hall *et al* skilfully demonstrate how certain groups created, sustained and transformed the moral panic about mugging. Thus, police groups seized the initiative, forming pre-emptive patrol groups even before the media bestowed a great deal of publicity. However, media coverage was certainly important in orchestrating public opinion and shaping public debate. But the main argument is that the association of mugging with the black presence in Britain was not simply accidental, a case of mistaken perceptions or unfortunate speculation. Rather, the moral panic was linked to the growing crisis of capitalism: '... the nature of the reaction to mugging can only be understood in terms of the way society – more especially the ruling-class alliances, the state apparatuses and the media – responded to a deepening economic, political and social crisis'. In particular, Hall *et al* focus on the crisis of 'hegemony'.

'Hegemony' (a term deriving from the Italian Marxist, Gramsci) draws attention to the ways in which ruling classes attempt to maintain their domination by ideological and cultural means. As well as exercising economic power and state coercion (police, military), the ruling class strive to win the hearts and minds of people and thereby gain 'consent' rather than mere obedience. However, this bid for hegemony is not always successful, and a crisis of hegemony occurs when there is a loss of faith in the social order, or when opposing groups challenge the legitimacy of the ruling groups. Hall *et al* chart the changing ways in which the state has struggled to secure hegemony in post-war Britain. In the early period of post-war growth and prosperity, hegemony was relatively successful, but the deepening problems of capitalism intensified, and in the 1960s hegemony was fractured by various social movements (student protests, youth culture, women's movement, industrial disorder, the rising waves of permissiveness, etc.). So a different 'control culture' emerged in order to re-establish authority, and the 'drift' of the state was arrested by a swing to 'law and order' (representing a move from 'consent' to 'legitimate coercion'). By focussing on such a potent symbol as 'law and order', the state was able to rally support for its campaign against not just muggers but also the wider forces of social unrest. The state was also able to capitalise on the symbolism of 'race', and that is why the identification of mugging with blacks was so important:

> ...the race theme was concrete and immediate... Their Saturday night parties were a constant reminder of the sacrifices demanded by the regime of work and the taboo on pleasure enshrined in the Protestant ethic. Their presence in the job queue recalled a century of unemployment and summary dismissal – evidence that a few years of 'full employment' cannot liquidate a whole class experience of economic insecurity. The black immigrant moved into the declining areas of the city, where Britain's 'forgotten Englishmen' lived on the very tightest of margins; he entered this 'tight little island' of white lower-middle and working class respectability – and, by his every trace, his looks, clothes, pigmentation, culture, mores and aspirations, announced his 'otherness'. His visible presence was a reminder of the unremitting squalor out of which that imperial noon had risen... The symbolism of the race-immigrant theme was resonant in its subliminal force, its capacity to set in motion the demons which haunt the collective subconscious of a 'superior race'; it triggered off images of sex, rape, primitivism, violence and excrement.

So the rich symbolism of the young black mugger was very powerful in its effects: in offending the latent 'sense of Englishness'; in connecting up with fears about 'youth today'; in offering a plausible explanation for the very real troubles people were experiencing; and in crystallising fears about 'inside conspiracies' by liberals who were imposing an alien presence and destroying valuable traditions and institutions. Race was certainly not the only symbol, but it brought together many of the preoccupations and fears of people living in a capitalist society experiencing deep crisis. Yet it enabled this crisis to be masked by a series of false resolutions (cries for law and order, desire for re-establishment of firm authority, stricter immigration legislation) which deflected attention away from the true source of the troubles. And in the process the moral panic inflamed racism and made life much harder for the scapegoated black communities in Britain.

Making Sense of Racism

The Marxist approach stresses features such as class conflict, labour exploitation and the history of capitalist expansion, and it attempts to uncover the economic forces which govern migration patterns and the emergence of racism. However, there are several variations on the basic Marxist themes, and different schools of thought debate the detailed factors and processes which underpin racism. A very crude Marxist account would run along the following lines: economic forces and conflicts are the main causes of racism; the origins of racism are directly attributable to the development of capitalism; racism performs vital functions for the capitalist system; an all-powerful state represents the economic interests of the dominant class by regulating the entry of coloured labour and by manipulating popular racism as the needs of capitalism dictate. However, the search for convincing evidence and for more sophisticated arguments tends to expose some of the weaknesses in the basic framework:

(1) There is a tendency to employ economic factors as a rigid formula to explain all aspects of race relations, and this under-estimates the role of other factors. Thus, Braham (1980) is probably correct in insisting that '. . . the dominant Marxist position appears to say little more than that racism is an ideology is a mechanical reflection of the mode of production of an economic base'. The independent force of ethnic, cultural and political factors is neglected by a Marxist approach which is obsessed with economic classes. The approach of Castles and Kosack, for example, not only loses sight of the ethnic affiliations of migrant labourers, but it also seems to dismiss 'racial' conflict as a matter of little interest. In recognition of these problems, some Marxists insist on the 'relative autonomy' of the economic, political and ideological spheres, but this tends to lead to rather untestable statements about the complex inter-relations of these three spheres.

(2) 'Conspiracy' versions usually describe a united ruling group which successfully manipulates racist feelings among the population. In reality, however, the dominant class is likely to be composed of competing interest groups or 'class fractions' whose short-term interests diverge. Thus, employers in low-growth industries may support immigration because it provides a cheap labour force; employers in prosperous industries may have no need for low-skill labour, and may oppose immigration because of fears of social unrest; and politicians have to balance the scales between economic pressures, political demands, and the desire to maintain good relations with New

Commonwealth countries. Similarly, it may be in the interests of the ruling groups to stir up racist feelings (in order to take advantage of blacks), but the same groups may support anti-discrimination legislation in order to prevent widespread social conflict. It can be seen, then, that a convincing conspiracy-type explanation needs to provide firm evidence on the dominant motives and actions of key groups: what, in fact, were their intentions? what interests were they promoting? how did they reconcile competing demands?

(3) More 'structuralist' versions of Marxism rely less on the intrigues of 'conspirators', and concentrate instead on the 'system needs' of capitalism. So it is argued that capitalism has certain broad system needs or requirements, and these needs mainly concern the establishment of conditions which assist the process of capital accumulation. Racism is seen as 'necessary', or at least useful, to capitalism, insofar as it performs the three previously-mentioned 'functions' (legitimisation, divide-and-rule, and scapegoating). Quite simply, racism arises because of its affinity with capitalist interests. However, there are certain problems with these structural explanations. Firstly, the identification of 'functions' does not demonstrate the initial 'causes' or 'origins' of racism, and so it is unwise to assume that racism was created precisely because of these intended functions. Secondly, it is not necessarily the case that the consequences of racism are indeed 'functional' for capitalists (e.g. the experience of racial prejudice can sharpen the political awareness of blacks and whites and lead to joint action against employers or politicians). Thirdly, the highly abstract level of the arguments lead to rather loose generalisations. For instance, the presumed 'connection' between capitalism and racism rests on a rather uncertain definition of 'capitalism' (which strangely includes the slave trade) and a special definition of 'racism' (which excludes the 'ethnocentrism' which existed before capitalism). Sweeping generalisations also overlook the diversity of views within and between racial groups, and they neglect the shift of racial attitudes over time. Finally, this structuralist approach is notoriously self-fulfilling and non-falsifiable (e.g. whether the state endorses racism or launches anti-discriminatory measures, arguments can be floated to show that this is in the interests of capitalism).

Many liberals would part company with the Marxist views that capitalism is inherently oppressive and exploitative, and that the class struggle is the major focus of attention. On the other hand, various elements of the Marxist approach to racism would be accepted by liberals and Weberians, and it is a caricature of liberalism to imagine that it pays no heed to economic issues or social conflicts. However, most liberals would shy clear of a unifying framework like Marxism, preferring to emphasise the multi-faceted nature of race issues. Some indication of this attitude is provided by Banton and Harwood (1975) who argue that:

> current notions of race are an integral part of the history of Western Europe, drawing upon many aspects of that story. These notions cannot be separated from the rest of that history and attributed to single factors like capitalism, colonialism, scientific error or personal prejudice. The sources of popular imagery concerning race are very diverse and the interrelations between their growth and contemporary political affairs are far too complex for the whole historical sequence to be explicable in simple terms.

The history of race relations is indeed a complex matter, but we hope that the models and theories covered in this book will help to shed some more light on this very important area.

Bibliography

Allen, S. *New Minorities, Old Conflicts* (Random House, New York, 1971).

Allport, G. *The Nature of Prejudice* (Addison-Wesley, Cambridge, Mass., 1954).

Ballard, R. 'Race and the Census' *New Society* 12 May 1983.

Ballard, R. and Ballard, C. 'The Sikhs: The Development of South Asian Settlements in Britain' in J. Watson, 1977.

Banton, M. *Race Relations* (Tavistock, London, 1967).

Banton, M. *The Idea of Race* (Tavistock, London, 1977).

Banton, M. 'Analytical and Folk Concepts of Race and Ethnicity' *Ethnic and Racial Studies* vol. 2 no. 2 April 1979.

Banton, M. and Harwood, J. *The Race Concept* (David and Charles, Newton Abbott, 1975).

Blauner, R. 'Black Culture: Myth or Reality?' in D. Bromley, 1972.

Bourne, J. 'Cheerleaders and Ombudsmen: The Sociology of Race Relations in Britain' *Race and Class* vol. 21 no. 4 1980.

Braham, P. *Class, Race and Immigration* (Open University Press, Milton Keynes, 1980).

Bromley, D. and Longino, C. (eds.) *White Racism and Black Americans* (Schenkman Pub. Co., Cambridge, Mass., 1970).

Brown, C. *Black and White in Britain: 3rd PSI Survey* (Heinemann, London, 1984).

Burgess, M. 'The resurgence of ethnicity' in *Ethnic and Racial Studies* vol. 1, 1978.

Carmichael, S. and Hamilton, C. *Black Power* (Penguin, Harmondsworth, 1969).

Cashmore, E. *Rastaman* (George Allen and Unwin, London, 1979).

Castles, S. and Kosack, G. *Immigrant Workers and Class Structure in Western Europe* (Oxford University Press, 1973).

Centre for Contemporary Cultural Studies. *The Empire Strikes Back* (Hutchinson, London, 1982).

Cohen, A. (ed.) *Urban Ethnicity* (Tavistock, London, 1974).

Community Relations Commission *Five Views of Multi-Racial Britain* (Commission for Racial Equality, London, 1978).

Cox. O. *Caste, Class and Race* (Monthly Review Press, New York, 1970).

Dahya, B. 'Pakistanis in Britain: Transients or Settlers?' *Race* vol. 14 no. 3 Jan. 1973.

Dahya, B. 'The Nature of Pakistani Ethnicity in Industrial Cities in Britain' in A. Cohen, 1974.

Daniel, W. W. *Racial Discrimination in England* (Penguin, Harmondsworth, 1968).

Dummett, M. and Dummett, A. 'The Role of Government in Britain's Racial Crisis' in C. Husband, 1982.

Eysenck, H. *Race, Intelligence and Education* (Maurice Temple Smith, London, 1971.

Field, S. *et al. Ethnic Minorities in Britain* (Home Office Research Study no. 68, London, 1981).

Field, S. *The Attitudes of Ethnic Minorities* (Home Office Research Study no. 80, London, 1984).

Fryer, P. *Staying Power* (Pluto Press, London, 1984).

Frank. A. G. *Capitalism and Underdevelopment in Latin America* (Monthly Review Press, New York, 1967).

Gans, H. 'Symbolic Ethnicity' *Ethnic and Racial Studies* vol. 2 no. 1 1979.

Glass, R. *Newcomers* (George Allen and Unwin, London, 1960).

Glazier, N. and Moynihan, D. (eds.) *Ethnicity: Theory and Experience* (Harvard University Press, 1975).

Goldthorpe, J. *The Sociology of the Third World* (Cambridge University Press, 1975).

Hall, S. *et al. Policing the Crisis* (Macmillan, London, 1978).

Hall, S. 'Racism and Reaction' in Community Relations Commission, 1978.

Hall, S. 'Race, Articulation and Societies Structured in Dominance' in UNESCO 1980.

Harrison, P. *Inside the Third World* (Penguin, Harmondsworth, 1979).

Hartmann, P. and Husband, C. *Racism and the Mass Media* (Davis-Poynter, London, 1974).

Hoogvelt, A. *The Sociology of Developing Societies* (Macmillan, London, 1976).

Horton, J. 'Order and Conflict Theories of Social Problems as Competing Ideologies'

American Journal of Sociology vol. LXXI no. 6 May 1966.

Husband, C. *White Media and Black Britain* (Arrow Books, London, 1975).

Husband, C. *'Race' in Britain* (Hutchinson, London, 1982).

Jenkins, R. Speech extract in *Race* vol. 8 no. 13 Jan. 1967.

Jensen, A. 'How Much Can We Boost I.Q. and Scholastic Achievement?' *Harvard Educational Review* 39, 1969.

Jowell, R. and Airey, C. *British Social Attitudes* (Social and Community Planning Research, 1984).

Kamin, L. *Intelligence: The Battle for the Mind* (Pan, London, 1981).

Khan, V. 'The Pakistanis: Mirpuri Villagers at Home and in Bradford' in J. Watson, 1977.

Krausz, E. *Ethnic Minorities in Britain* (Paladin, London, 1971).

Layton-Henry, Z. *The Politics of Race in Britain* (George Allen and Unwin, London, 1984).

Lea, J. and Young, J. *What is to be done about Law and Order?* (Penguin, Harmondsworth, 1984).

Lyon, M. 'Race and Ethnicity in Pluralistic Societies' *New Community* vol. 1 no. 4 Summer 1972.

Mason, D. 'After Scarman: A Note on the Concept of Institutional Racism' *New Community* vol. 10 no. 1 Summer 1982.

McKay, J. 'Primordial and Mobilisationist Approaches to Ethnic Phenomena' *Ethnic and Racial Studies* vol. 5 no. 4 1982.

Miles, R. *Racism and Migrant Labour* (Routledge & Kegan Paul, London, 1982).

Moore, R. *Racism and Black Resistance in Britain* (Pluto Press, London, 1975).

Parekh, B. 'Asians in Britain: Problem or Opportunity?' in Community Relations Commission, 1978.

Park, R. *Race and Culture* (Free Press, Glencoe, 1950).

Parmar, P. 'Gender, Race and Class: Asian Women in Resistance' in Centre For Contemporary Cultural Studies, 1982.

Patterson, S. *Dark Strangers* (Penguin, Harmondsworth, 1965).

Policy Studies Institute. *Police and People in London* (PSI, London, 1983).

Pryce, K. *Endless Pressure* (Penguin, Harmondsworth, 1979).

Rex, J. *Race Relations in Sociological Theory* (Weidenfeld and Nicholson, London, 1970).

Rex, J. *Race, Colonialism and the City* (Routledge & Kegan Paul, London, 1973).

Rex, J. 'Race in the Inner City' in Community Relations Commission, 1978.

Rex, J. and Moore, R. *Race, Community and Conflict* (Oxford University Press, 1967).

Rex, J. and Tomlinson, S. *Colonial Immigrants in a British City* (Routledge & Kegan Paul, London, 1979).

Rose, E. *et al. Colour and Citizenship* (Oxford University Press, 1969).

Scarman Report. *The Brixton Disorders 10–12 April 1981* (HMSO, 1981).

Schermerhorn, R. *Comparative Ethnic Relations* (Random House, New York, 1970).

Smith, D. *Racial Disadvantage in Britain: The P.E.P. Report* (Penguin, Harmondsworth, 1977).

Social Trends 1983 and 1984 (HMSO).

Taylor, S. 'Riots: Some Explanations' *New Community* vol. 9 no. 2 Autumn 1981.

UNESCO 'Moscow Declaration 1964' *Race* vol. 6 no. 3 Jan. 1965.

UNESCO *4th Statement on Race and Racial Prejudice* (UNESCO, Paris, 1967).

UNESCO *Sociological Theories: Race and Colonialism* (UNESCO, Paris, 1980).

Van Den Berghe, P. 'Race and Ethnicity' *Ethnic and Racial Studies* vol. 1 1978.

Watson, J. *Between Two Cultures* (Basil Blackwell, London, 1977).

Walvin, J. *Black and White* (Allen Lane, London, 1973).

Walvin, J. *Passage to Britain* (Penguin, Harmondsworth, 1984).

Westergaard, J. and Resler, H. *Class in a Capitalist Society* (Penguin, Harmondsworth, 1976).

Yinger, M. 'Toward a Theory of Assimilation and Dissimilation' *Ethnic and Racial Studies* vol. 4 no. 3 1981.

Young, J. and Lea, J. 'Urban Violence and Political Marginalisation' *Critical Social Policy* vol. 1 no. 3 Spring 1982.

Index